God's Plan
for the Church—
GROWTH!

Michael Hamilton

Radiant BOOKS
Gospel Publishing House/Springfield. Mo. 65802

02-0885

Library of Congress Catalog Card Number 81-82021
International Standard Book Number 0-88243-885-9
Printed in the United States of America

A teacher's guide for individual or group study with this book is available from the Gospel Publishing House.

Contents

1

Pattern for Church Growth

"It is God's will for the Church to grow; that His lost children be found," stated Donald McGavern in a recent church growth meeting in Pasadena, California. That statement, coupled with events around us, reminds the church that this is a time perhaps greater than any other in which to "grow a church."

Many crises affect the world today. The energy crisis costs the individual both money and pleasure. Worldwide hunger is a growing problem. Leadership crises, both nationally and internationally, cause concern in the hearts of many. In these difficult times, the Church has its greatest opportunity.

Churches all across America are growing. City and suburban churches are growing. Rural churches thought to be dead a few years ago are experiencing a rebirth. Every region of the country gives evidence that the Church is alive and well.

In spite of regional distinctives and operational differences, are there basics to church growth in the 1980s? Is there a New Testament pattern to follow?

Our best example could come from the first church in Jerusalem.

Those first members of the Church were faced

with a monumental task. They were living in a hostile world. Religious leaders of the day were threatened by the presence of this new movement. The Roman government was intolerant of any potential challenge. There was uncertainty in their future.

This first church grew at a phenomenal rate. They grew from 120 in the Upper Room to 3,000 following Peter's sermon at Pentecost. This early church continued to grow in Jerusalem and Antioch. It spread to Ephesus and Rome. The challenge of the first-century church is our challenge today.

Acts 2 gives basic ingredients of New Testament church growth. Let's consider some of the factors that made this church grow.

Unity

It was a unified church. There is strength in numbers. The Bible says: "They were in one accord in one place." Acts 2:46 states that they *continued* daily in one accord. Now that's not always easy. It is one thing to start out in the same frame of mind; it is another to stay that way!

Jesus' followers were of one accord as they waited patiently for the enduement of power from the Holy Spirit. They were of one mind as Peter preached, believers testified, and 3,000 souls were added to the Church. They were of one spirit when, in Acts 12, Peter was taken prisoner by King Herod. Can you imagine the excitement the believers felt when Peter came into their midst as a direct answer to their prayers?

Several years ago, I had the opportunity to preach a missionary revival in South America. I was overwhelmed by the warmth and friendliness of the people. Their strength and solidarity also amazed me.

Near the end of the second week of meetings, however, a rather frightening incident occurred. I was getting ready to preach when the pastor noticed a large crowd of people had gathered outside the preaching station. He asked me to step outside and advised me that a group of people were having a voodoo service and attempting to cast a spell on our meeting! Now that got the attention of this preacher right away! I must admit the crowd was frightening.

When we went back inside, I noticed a group of men, women, and young people standing behind the pulpit area where I would soon be preaching. "Why are they here?" I asked the pastor. He told me they were going to *stand with me* during the preaching. Needless to say, we had an anointed service that night.

Wouldn't it be great if all pastors and teachers felt that kind of solid, unified commitment as they shared the Word?

In these exciting and difficult days, the church that lives in unity as brothers and sisters will be a growing church.

Gladness (Joy)

Joy or gladness is a fruit of the Spirit. This spiritual quality was also in evidence in the lives of the members of the Early Church. Being joyful is easy when everything is going right. But a "supernatural" kind of joy is needed at other times and is helpful to our lives. The Word says they were able to "eat their meat with gladness" as they did the work of the Lord. Joy is contagious.

I visited a church like this recently. Walking into the foyer, I could sense an almost supernatural happiness. Many folks were smiling and enjoying one another's company. Before newcomers noticed, they had been drawn into wonderful fellowship. During that service, we laughed and cried and hugged one another. I came away from that place exhausted but genuinely happy.

This special quality uplifts individuals and congregations. It makes people want to be together. The joy of the Lord helped the Early Church find favor with men. It does the same thing for you and me today.

Obedience

The Early Church was an obedient church. The Bible says in 1 Samuel 15:22: "To obey is better than sacrifice." We are all part of God's plan. We may not understand the whole picture, but God does. As obedient children we must learn to do those things that are pleasing to the Lord and His purposes.

Early Church fathers may have thought they had a better plan for fulfilling the Great Commission than going to the Gentiles. It had never been done before. Other members of the congregation might not understand. It took the miracle in Cornelius' life and a heavenly vision to touch Peter. Others may have found it difficult to accept Peter's actions. But Peter obeyed, and God brought an increase. On a similar subject, Paul could say to King Agrippa: "I was not disobedient unto the heavenly vision" (Acts

26:19). If the Church is to flourish today, it must be obedient to God's plan.

This could mean a change in direction or emphasis for the church. It might mean a sacrifice of time, talent, or money. Today, as in the Early Church, there is great fulfillment in obedience to God's plan for the Church.

Knowledge

"They continued steadfastly in the apostles' doctrine" (Acts 2:42). Some members of the Early Church got into a lot of trouble because they were not knowledgeable about God's plan for the Church. They became involved in Gnosticism, Arianism, and other ideologies and philosophies that were contrary to the teachings of Christ.

This is a problem facing the Church today. Cult worship, self-proclaimed messiahs, and so-called "gospel superstars" have, at times, brought injury to the body of Christ. Many churches have found themselves in a credibility crisis. They have asked the question: "Who can we believe?" The Church must be sure of its fundamental beliefs.

Levels of knowledge are increasing all over the world. Children are learning to read at a much younger age than ever before. High school and college-age people are involved in mind-expanding studies. Adults have again discovered new educational opportunities. It has been reported that there are presently more adults enrolled in continuing education classes than all school-age and college students combined. The Church must be constantly involved in producing solid Bible knowledge. The church that grows will be an informed church, knowledgeable in God's Word and aware of God's plan for their lives.

The apostles were seeking and living God's truth. They provided a basic foundation for belief. That is one reason why their churches grew.

Fellowship

The Early Church was a fellowshipping church. They spent time together in fellowship and in breaking of bread. Fellowship with brothers and sisters and communion with God are a vital part of church growth.

Think about this: Do you know your neighbors on both sides and in back of your residence? If you're like most of us, you don't. We are sometimes so busy that we fail to have contact with the people we could influence the most.

Many people are suffering from loneliness. They are frustrated; not knowing how to build close relationships with others. The hectic pace of our lifestyle further alienates people. How can we build personal relationships in a growing congregation?

The Early Church enjoyed large meetings. Peter preached to 3,000 souls on one occasion and over 5,000 on another. Peter also made use of home groups to establish spiritual relationships. Acts 5:42 states: "And daily in the temple, and in every house, they ceased not to teach and preach Jesus Christ." The believers used home groups for instruction, edification, and fellowship.

Dick Foth, president of Bethany Bible College, gives direction for small-group meetings by using the "WIFE" principle. It can be stated as follows:

Worship	A major purpose for gathering together is to share worship. As we commune with the Lord, we can increase our knowledge and awareness of each other.
Instruction	Involvement in God's Word is vital. Without a foundation in faith, any group will die.
Fellowship	We need one another. As we fellowship together, we build spiritual bridges of commitment to one another.
Expression (Prayer)	It is a privilege to pray for our brothers and sisters. Paul said, "Brethren, pray for us." He felt the need to give and receive this kind of expression.

There is no need for loneliness in the growing, glowing body of Christ.

Prayer

The first church was brought into being in a prayer meeting. Believers were praying in the Upper Room as the outpouring of the Holy Spirit ushered in a new day. They were in prayer at Peter's first evangelistic crusade where 3,000 souls were added to the Church. Peter and John were going to a prayer meeting when they came upon the lame man at the gate of the temple. Prayer strengthened the Early Church during persecution and the Dispersion. Jesus himself said that some things come only through prayer and fasting.

Churches that are growing today are constantly being drawn to prayer. They are praying for growth, but also for the multitude of needs that come as a result of that growth.

James, the brother of the Lord, speaks to the Church on the subject of prayer: "The effectual fervent prayer of a righteous man availeth much" (James 5:16). Prayer is a great growth tool of the church today.

Praises

One last ingredient helps us put the growth puzzle of the Early Church together—praise. It is a good thing to offer praise unto God.

Jesus gave an example of praise when Lazarus was sick. Martha and Mary called for Jesus to come. But when He arrived, Lazarus had already died and the family had gone into mourning. Picture the scene as Jesus went to the tomb and requested that it be opened. He then set the example of praise. In John 11:41, Jesus said, "I thank thee that thou hast heard me." Jesus was about to perform a wonderful miracle. But before He did that He offered praise.

Paul and Silas followed Christ's pattern. Acts 16:25 relates: "At midnight Paul and Silas prayed, and sang praises unto God: and the prisoners heard them." The Early Church found favor with God and man as they were continually praising and giving thanks.

The opportunity for praise sets the stage for bigger and better things to come. Peter and John, Paul and Silas, the lame man at the gate—these and others learned the value of this kind of dialogue with the Lord.

Today, a church that allows itself the freedom to enter into praise is in most cases a church that is moving forward. The openness in heart and spirit, and the warmth that comes from sharing good things with others, affect both the members and newcomers that enter the doors of the church. Praise is a powerful ingredient to add to the growth of the church.

So growth patterns of the Early Church come into view. In the first church we see a group of people who had one goal—to reach the lost. The unity of this group was tested from within and without. They stood in one accord. They were joyful in spirit and obedient. They were informed, not just following tradition, and they were committed to one another in fellowship. The Early Church knew how to pray and when to praise. This first church made an impact on the world.

We have not only an example for today, but also a fresh challenge. It is God's will for the Church to grow. It may be necessary for us to reevaluate our position: Have I found my place in the local body of Christ? Am I contributing my special talents and gifts to the work of the Kingdom? Do I understand the impact of God's Great Commission on my life and my need to reach out in evangelism? Am I now expressing the joy of the Lord in my personal life and in group activities? Has my prayer life contributed to the overall health of the body of believers? Does the community around me hear praise coming from my lips?

In the following chapters, we will discuss the answers to some of these questions in relation to the New Testament pattern for church growth.

13

2

God's Concern for the Lost

"You don't care what happens to me. Even God doesn't care for me anymore!" Linda looked across the desk with tears in her eyes. She was having problems in her home and had sought my help. But her greatest need was a new relationship with Christ. This young lady was a 21-year-old wife, mother, and church attender who had come to feel that God didn't care for her anymore. She is not alone in her feelings. Countless persons feel that God really doesn't care. But He *does* care for us.

There is much evidence to show God's concern for the lost. As early as Genesis, God was reaching to man with redemption. Verse after verse of Old and New Testament passages show God's repeated attempts to reach man. The ultimate act of love is giving, and God has given and still gives from His concern for the lost.

If we are truly to understand God's concern for the lost, we must see people as God sees them. A few questions come to mind: What do lost persons look like? How lost are they? What is our responsibility to the lost?

Let's consider how the lost person appears to us. He may be a businessman or a doctor. She may teach school or be a faithful mother. As we see these successful individuals, young or old, it is sometimes difficult to imagine them as being lost. One pastor said it well, "It's hard to tell my banker that he has no hope." We may let physical or material surroundings cloud our vision of important things. How does God really see people?

God sees us without all the pomp, dignity, and self-confidence that we may think we possess. He sees us as children in need of eternal help. God cares deeply about lost persons.

During a recent military conflict, a Christian lady went to her pastor, broken and troubled. She had just lost her son in battle. She began to pour out her soul to her pastor. "How do you think God felt when my son was killed?" she asked. The pastor thought for a moment and replied, "I imagine He felt just like He did when His Son was killed."

God has a high stake in lost persons. He gave His Son that they might live. God sees the lost person as we must see him: desperately in need of life-changing help.

How Lost Are the Lost?

Dr. Win Arn, in the book *Ten Steps for Church Growth,* states:

> We remind ourselves constantly that people without Jesus Christ are really lost. The only way people can come to the Father is by Jesus Christ (Winfield C. Arn and Donald A. McGavran [New York: Harper & Row Publishers, Inc., 1977]).

Even though most church people believe that those outside Christ are lost, many fail to move beyond that point. The breakdown comes in the thinking, planning, and promoting that's necessary to reach them. It is important for us to have a Biblical understanding of man's lost state and to realize his total helplessness without Christ. It is very simple: God wants lost people to be found.

What Is Our Responsibility to the Lost?

First, we must be committed to touching lost persons with our prayers.

God's Word advises us to "pray . . . the Lord of the harvest, that he would send forth laborers into his harvest" (Luke 10:2). We need to pray for world evangelism. There are millions of people with whom we will never personally come in contact, yet we must share the burden for reaching them with the gospel. We also have the responsibility of winning the lost in our own ministry area. Possibly the most winnable people we will ever meet live in our own community. Some of these people will never be reached unless we reach out to them.

Our second responsibility is to live a life of testimony before the lost.

In Romans 12:1, 2, Paul says:

> I beseech you therefore, brethren, by the mercies of God, that ye present your bodies a living sacrifice, holy, acceptable unto God, which is your reasonable service. And be not conformed to this world: but be ye transformed by the renewing of your mind, that ye may prove what is that good, and acceptable, and perfect will of God.

Our service and our responsibility do not end with prayer, but continue in our daily lives before the world. How does that lost person view us? Are our lives a help or hindrance to his accepting the gospel? Are our attitudes and actions consistent with Christian values? The manner in which we live may determine whether or not our lost friends are found in Christ.

Our third responsibility is to plan, think, and promote for an increase.

There are things we can do to help prepare the way for lost persons to be found. Consider some of the following.

We Must Find the Bridges of God

Donald McGavran, a missionary to India in the early 1930s, discovered a growth principle that was to have great impact on all future church growth evangelism. He called it finding the bridges of God. The premise is that churches grow faster as they reach out to people with whom members already have contact in their existing social network.

A pastor from the Midwest related the following incident:

"Seven-year-old Danny and his mother, father, and grandparents moved to our town in 1972. They were from Latin America and spoke very little English. They also had many customs that were different from those of our community. Living in a small Midwestern town did not promise to be a pleasurable experience for this family.

"Danny came to Sunday school because of a vacation Bible school announcement in the newspaper. He liked the singing and colorful stories, and he started attending regularly on Sunday mornings. His parents, although Catholic, allowed him to attend. They thought the classes would improve his English. During a children's Sunday school contest, the boys and girls were asked to bring as many friends as possible to Sunday school. But Danny didn't have any little friends, so he invited his mother. She came with him one Sunday morning and gave her heart to the Lord. The following Sunday he brought his father. He, too, gave his heart to Jesus. Before the month had passed, Danny's mother, father, and grandparents had been saved. A letter was written to family members in Argentina and several relatives were exposed to the Pentecostal witness.''

Danny was only a little boy, but he was a "bridge" to folks who otherwise would have been unreachable. Today this family is active in the local church. They have been accepted in the community. Doors are open to them that would have remained closed for many years. But most important, they have met Christ.

The "bridges of God" principle is a New Testament principle. Andrew, after meeting Jesus, went to get his brother, so he too could experience a life change. Others also followed this New Testament pattern.

We are living in a time of mistrust. People are cautious about giving of themselves to anyone or anything. We must find common ground in reaching people. Bridges described here may arise from a work experience, a common need, or an achievement. Family ties, social structure, or educational background may help build the bridge. Churches and individuals are making this principle work. Can you see the excitement as a nucleus of people reach out to surrounding areas? This principle results in a continuing program of people relating with one another.

An interesting survey was conducted recently by the Institute for American Church Growth. Several denominations were contacted and 10,000 people were interviewed. They were asked the question: "Why did you attend your church for the first time?" The results of the survey were broken down as follows:

Just walked in—3%
Attracted by a program—2-4%
Pastor—3-5%
Special event—2-3%
Visitation—1-2%
Sunday school—3-5%
Crusade—.001%
Friends and relatives—70-90%

These results do not mean that programs such as Sunday school and visitation are not workable today. On the contrary, they are a major cause of growth. These figures simply reveal that already-established contacts build bridges that we can use to reach the lost.

This bridging theory was illustrated to me personally a few years ago while I was pastoring in Kansas City, Missouri. Our church was involved in a bus ministry. Newcomers were attending the church every Sunday. Our contact list was being enlarged.

One Sunday, a young lady and her daughter came to the morning service, but I never got to meet them personally. Then, only 2 days after visiting our church, a terrible tragedy struck their home. This young woman's husband was killed right before her eyes. The church ministered to her and I was asked to preach the funeral. Even though she had visited our church just once a few days before, she had a need that only a caring, concerned group of people could meet. I remember her words at the graveside, "Pastor, I couldn't have made it without the church this week." She was later saved, along with her daughter. Had that bridge not been built, we would have missed an opportunity to minister. We must find the bridge to those in our area of ministry.

We Must Develop a Church Growth Consciousness

This, simply stated, means determining in our own hearts that it is God's will for the church to grow, and applying our efforts and planning to encourage that growth. In the past, time, effort, and money have in some cases been spent on nonproductive programs. This may have been because of tradition or perhaps because we didn't know any better. As we develop a concern for church growth, we will see the need to apply our energies to winning the lost and helping the believer mature. All other concerns will fall into second place in our thinking. Programs, buildings, and so forth will be centered on meeting and reaching people.

There are some things that we must do to grow. Perhaps we may also have to lay aside a few things to continue to grow. An active church that is growth conscious reminds us of our reason for being. A church growth consciousness serves as a continual reminder that we must have lost persons in view as we plan daily activities, and we must balance maintenance ministries with outreach ministries.

We Must See Our Community Through "Church Growth Eyes"

An optimist is an individual who, when looking at his gas gauge, sees it as half *full*. A pessimist, on the other hand, sees it as half *empty*. (A fool doesn't see it at all because he doesn't look at it!)

There are unlimited opportunities of ministry as we look through "church growth eyes." The Institute for American Church Growth gives this definition: "Church Growth Eyes is a characteristic of Christians who have achieved an ability to see the possibilities for growth and to apply appropriate strategies to gain maximum results for Christ and His Church."

The individual with "church growth eyes" can look at his ministry area and see needs. He can also see ways of meeting and fulfilling those needs. One healthy sign of a church with "church growth eyes" is that it continually looks for new outreach ministries. Church growth eyes allow you to reach into areas beyond the traditional Sunday school or worship service. This ministry may include apartment house evangelism, neighborhood Bible clubs, a booth at the fair, radio or television advertising, or elective classes that deal with special needs. With church growth eyes, you can determine the needs of your community.

Sam and Jeannie Mayo pastor the Assemblies of God church in Bellevue, Nebraska (as of this writing). Bellevue is an Air Force town. More than 50 percent of the 1,000-plus congregation come from the Strategic Air Command Air Force Base located there.

Many young mothers of the church expressed concern over certain aspects of child rearing. These mothers were from all parts of the country. They were far away from their own parents and needed advice on toilet training their small children. Jeannie, through church growth eyes, saw a need and the opportunity to reach young families. She arranged for some of the "grandmas" of the church to give a class on toilet training small children. Many grateful unchurched mothers had their first contact with the church through this program of concern.

When we hear church growth eyes mentioned we may think only of numbers. While I was traveling from New York to St. Louis recently, I met a minister on the plane who commented on church growth. He said, "Church growth to me is just getting bigger and bigger. Why don't you ever mention some other ways a church can grow?" He was right. There are different kinds of church growth.

Internal Growth

This can be described as the growth of the body of believers—church health. It has been suggested that if we spent as much time praying for the health of our church as we do for our physical bodies, our internal structure would benefit. Internal growth speaks of loving, caring concern among believers as they minister to one another.

Expansion Growth

This is the growth of the church by reaching lost persons. Expansion growth is directly related to fulfilling the Great Commission to go to the whole world.

Extension Growth

Basically this is the planting of new churches. More will be said about church planting in a later chapter.

Bridging Growth

This is establishing new churches in significantly different cultural and geographical areas. It is done on the mission field, but it may also be needed in your area of ministry. Special groups, such as language groups, may need your help if they are to be reached for Christ.

Prophetic eyes allowed Ezekiel to look at dead and decaying bones and see an army. Church growth eyes allowed Paul to feel hope for a struggling Corinthian church. This same spiritual insight allows leadership to look at things as they are and see great possibilities for growth.

Possibilities for growth exist in the inner city and in rural America. There are opportunities for outreach in suburbia and in the small town. As the anointing of the Spirit opens our spiritual eyes, new opportunities will be born.

Now we go back to the young lady's question, "Do you care? Does God really care for me?" The answer is, "Yes." God is concerned for the lost. As we see people the way God sees them, through church growth eyes, we will be challenged as never before to reach the lost.

3

God Really Cares About the Church

My first experience in pastoring a church could only be described as a comedy of errors. At 21 years of age, having spent 1 year as an assistant pastor, I felt I was ready. It would take too long to list all the things I didn't know about pastoring. One story will suffice.

After about 3 months of pastoring, it was time to have a baptismal service. That was something I had never participated in before. Three candidates presented themselves for water baptism. My father, who had pastored for 37 years, called to give me last-minute instructions. He told me where to stand and what to say. I was ready. Everything had been done and the candidates presented themselves at the baptismal tank.

Candidates one and two came and went without any problem. Candidate number three was a sweet little lady who had been saved about 2 weeks. Nobody had told me she was afraid of water. She entered the water and we started to struggle. As she was going down into the water, she kicked, causing me to lose my balance. Now this baptism was a first for me and I wanted it to go right. When she came out of the water, I noticed that the top of her head was still as dry as mine. I could see the reports going to my district office: "This new pastor does not immerse baptismal candidates." She had stopped struggling now, thinking we were through. I saw my chance and dunked her when she wasn't expecting it! A scriptural crisis had been averted! That's about how much I knew about pastoring.

That little church grew, and with moderate growth came the typical problems every church faces. I was unprepared for the meeting that my only deacon called one night. "I don't like the way things are going," he said. "I'm going to starve you out."

His support was the major support of that little church, so I believed him. I had not yet come to realize God's deep concern for His church. I wasn't sure what God could do about the situation. Had I known a little more about God's watchcare and concern for His church, we both would have been better off. As a result, I left that church before my time.

God does care for His church—both the collective Body and the individuals within the Body. In the Book of Ephesians, Paul, speaking under the anointing of the Spirit, has much to say about God's concern for the Church:

> Husbands, love your wives, even as Christ also loved the church, and gave himself for it; that he might sanctify and cleanse it with the washing of water by the word, that he might present it to himself a glorious church, not having spot, or wrinkle, or any such thing; but that it should be holy and without blemish. So ought men to love their wives as their own bodies. He that loveth his wife loveth himself (5:25-28).

God Loves the Church Collectively

There is a basic position of honor and authority

that God has given to the local church. Jesus said: "Where two or three are gathered together in my name, there am I in the midst of them" (Matthew 18:20). What greater honor could be bestowed upon the Church than for Christ to be present?

Let us consider some of those special benefits Christ has given the Church.

He Has Given His Love

Christ says, "I love you," to the Church. We see and do things differently when we love someone. Just a few weeks ago, I saw a couple that was genuinely in love. They were in their middle sixties and had been married for 40 years. There was a closeness about them that is rare. In fact, they even almost looked like one another! This beautiful couple was still attempting to please each other. I noticed a few other things about them too, such as the way each built the other up. It was evident that they protected and looked after one another.

That's the way Christ loves the Church. He gave himself for us. He looks beyond our faults and sees the potential we may not see. He shows His love to us; we have a love relationship with Him. Christ says to His church, "I love you and have given Myself just for you."

Make Me Better, Please

A little boy came up to me the other day after a sermon and said, "Mister, make me better, please." Now I cannot do that. Christ can. The Scriptures say He gave himself that He might sanctify us. This must have been the experience King David was looking for when he said: "Search me, O God, and know my heart: try me, and know my thoughts: and see if there be any wicked way in me, and lead me in the way everlasting" (Psalm 139:23, 24).

Sanctification is not automatic. It is Christ's purpose to sanctify the Church in love, but we must be willing to be involved in the process: "Present your bodies a living sacrifice, holy, acceptable unto God, which is your reasonable service" (Romans 12:1). Paul could urge this "living sacrifice" because it was "good" for the Church.

I saw a bumper sticker recently that said, "I'm not perfect—yet." Another sign said, "If our church were perfect, you wouldn't be able to attend." Think about that one. Many of us are caught in the position of the little boy—looking for someone or something that can make us better. As a church we are striving to, as Paul said, "be perfected." We can be thankful that God is concerned about the Church and is perfecting it daily.

"Can I have my snack now?" That's a favorite question around our house. It wouldn't seem like the Hamilton residence if Jennie and Jamie didn't come in just before bedtime and repeat those words. Every night they must have a snack. Our children receive good food. They eat some things that they don't even like because they're good for them. Their snack time is more of a "love feast." The expression *love feast* may seem a bit heavy, but their snack is a little "I-love-you" nourishment.

Dr. Anthony Palma, former Dean of Theology of the Assemblies of God Graduate School in Springfield, Missouri, says: "The words *nourish* and *cherish* in the Greek are closely related. They have similar meaning and kinship." God shows His concern as He gives nourishment to the Church. He loves to give warmth to the Church. This is a little like that bedtime snack.

God Is Concerned About the Welfare of the Individual

What about the individual worker in the church? We frequently hear about workers who become "burned out." Does God care about the individual worker? Yes, He does. There are many helps directed from heaven toward the workers: love, satisfaction, peace, a sense of accomplishment, and more.

One thing that seems to be at a premium today is time. In recent years I have found myself praying a prayer for the worker: "Lord, multiply their time. As they work for You, stretch their hours. Give them more time for their family and the things they like to do." Several workers have told me that they feel this blessing of time. Perhaps it is better management, but I like to think that God gives time back to people.

"You promised me!" How many times have you heard that said? With all the benefits God gives the Church, there are also specific promises He has given the individual worker. Let's look at some of the promises.

Promise of His Presence

Matthew 28:20 gives Jesus' promise to be with us always. What a comfort in the midst of a crisis or confusion to know that He is there!

Warner Miles, missionary to Korea, told of the problems the missionaries faced while helping some Korean orphans. Fear, mistrust, hunger, and other disorders caused the children serious problems.

Brother Miles stated that one particular group of children was having trouble getting to sleep at night. They had come from an area where many were starving. They would restlessly lie awake at night, crying far into the morning hours. One of the medical staff had an idea. "Give the children a piece of bread. Tell them not to eat it. If they get hungry, we will give them another piece to eat. They should save this piece for tomorrow." This solved their problem. The children knew they would have something to eat the next day.

Sometimes we may be like those children. Hunger, concern for loved ones, and other problems may cause us distress. But being able to hold onto the Bread of Life tells us there will be something for tomorrow. The promise of His presence is a great joy for the worker.

Promise of Victory

God reminded Joshua: "Every place that the sole of your foot shall tread upon, that have I given unto you" (Joshua 1:3). Everybody likes to win. These words of encouragement to Joshua are also good news to the worker as he claims God's promises. Notice how the promise of victory is worded. We are not promised just what we sit and dream about, but what we are willing to *reach out* and *claim*.

I knew a young man who tried an experiment. He was a bus captain for a growing Assemblies of God church. This man was struggling on his bus route with only 20 to 30 children each Sunday. By his own testimony, he confessed that he got nervous when he talked to people. One Sunday, his bus was late in arriving at Sunday school. When it finally pulled up at the church, 100 children and adults climbed out!

Later, the pastor asked the bus captain, "What happened to our bus route? Where did all those people come from?" The young man replied, "I figured that God loved me as much as He loved Joshua." Then he explained that each night after work, he had walked along his bus route praying, "Lord, give me this house. Lord, give me these people." He had knocked on many doors, and God had simply given him what he had asked for. I am not recommending this method for everyone, but his commitment is something to note. For those who are willing to step out in faith, victory is promised.

Promise of Holy Spirit Illumination

In John 14:26 we are promised the help of the Spirit as we minister: "He shall teach you all things, and bring all things to your remembrance." The Pentecostal believer has a great asset here. The fresh anointing of the Spirit does make a difference. This Holy Spirit illumination will be a help in witnessing, in ministering to needs, and in other ways.

Elisha knew of the promise of the Holy Spirit. Elijah asked him, "What can I do for you when I go?" Elisha replied with the oft-quoted phrase, "Let a double portion of thy spirit be upon me." It was the dynamic of the Holy Spirit that caused Elisha to touch many lives. As we accept the promise of the Spirit, we can touch those around us for Christ. Church growth helps, combined with the power of Pentecost, make an unbeatable combination.

Promise of Answered Prayer

First John 5:14 states that if we ask anything

according to His will, "He heareth us." For the church growth person concerned for the lost, no promise holds greater joy than the promise of answered prayer. It is God's will for the Church to grow. It is God's will for lost persons to be found. It is God's will for believers to mature and flourish in Christ. What an assurance to know that if we ask for these things, He will hear us. When God hears us, we know that He will answer our request.

Kenneth Brown, current pastor of People's Church in Arnold, Missouri, has been a church growth pastor for a number of years. Pastor Brown went to Arnold, Missouri, when there was no strong Assemblies of God work there. For a few years, he struggled, trying to make his church grow, but nothing seemed to work. Finally he decided to start praying specifically for things related to growth. By asking from the Lord, he was able to put certain growth principles into action. Today, People's Church is one of the strongest Assemblies of God churches in the Midwest. It is a wonderful comfort to know that God hears and answers our prayers.

Promise of Sowing and Reaping

"They that sow in tears shall reap in joy" (Psalm 126:5). Another Scripture verse (which is often used in judgment) is Galatians 6:7: "Be not deceived; God is not mocked: for whatsoever a man soweth, that shall he also reap." This verse is also a growth promise to the Church. The farmer knows that he must sow grain to reap a harvest. Likewise, the businessman spends money to make money. The church growth person must give of himself—of his time, talent, and money—to see growth. God *always* gives an increase. The Bible says that if we sow we shall reap. It is a promise. Churches that are growing probably have more sowers in the field.

Promise of Fulfillment

"He that loseth his life for my sake shall find it." This verse seems to be a contradiction. How can I find fulfillment by giving up those things that are important to me? True fulfillment will not come from pushing, shoving, and fighting to get to the top. Too many individuals have fought so hard, only to realize their prize wasn't worth the effort. Paul could speak to that subject. In Philippians 3:7,8, he states: "What things were gain to me, those I counted loss for Christ. . . . I count all things but loss . . . that I may win Christ." It seems hard to believe, but in losing, we win.

Bob attended the church where I was the youth pastor for a time. He was a high school football player. This boy showed the promise of one day being good enough to play professional football. Then Bob felt a call to the ministry. His father, however, was against it. "You're going to play football," he said on many occasions.

This young man came to a personal crisis. He would have to give up much if he answered the call to the ministry. But Bob decided to obey the Lord anyway. He truly did lose his personal life in his attempt to find himself in Christ. His father could not understand his decision. He moved the family to another town to get Bob away from the influence of the church. Several difficult years followed.

Not long ago, I was on a church growth tour in the state of Iowa when a young man and his family approached me after one of the services. It was Bob. He was now pastoring his first little church. In losing his personal life, he had found a better, more fulfilling one. We have the promise of personal fulfillment as we lose ourselves in Christ.

My daughter Jennifer taught me the worth of a promise a few years ago. Several months before her birthday, she told us what she wanted. "Dad, I want a canopy bed." Just a few days before her birthday, however, I realized I would be out of the country on a preaching mission when her birthday came. I called Jenny in to sit on my lap. "Jenny, when your birthday comes, Dad will be a long way from here." She looked up at me and said, "Dad, it's all right." I told her that I might not even be able to call her. She said, "Dad, I'm not worried about the bed. You made me a promise and you always keep your promises." If we as parents love our children and try to keep our promises, how much more will our Heavenly Father keep His promises to us.

God loves His church. He has pledged His trust to the Church. He has given it a rightful place of authority in this world. He has made promises to us through His Word. He loves you as an individual worker. The resources of heaven are available to help us as we work for Him.

4

Finding Your Place

Candid students of the New Testament are compelled to admit that the "one-man ministry" so generally prevailing among the churches today is *not* the divine order as therein revealed" (Donald Gee, *Concerning Spiritual Gifts* [Springfield, MO: Gospel Publishing House, rev. 1980], p. 27).

Donald Gee made the above statement to stress the need for members' involvement in the ministry of the local church. Much has been accomplished since that time both to the credit and the failing of the church. On the one hand, the church has grown so that it touches almost the entire spectrum of life. Church membership is popular. Countless thousands have been won to Christ. Every sign points to the continued good health of the church that is established on Biblical principles.

On the other hand, some congregations are now depending solely on the "professional minister" to do the jobs of soul winning, showing hospitality, ministering in music, and other ministries associated with the church. There is a need and a place for the trained, educated, and gifted full-time man or woman of God. But there is also a need for gifted lay persons to fill ministry opportunities in the local church. Until a few years ago, very little had been written on the subject of spiritual gifts. With the charismatic renewal and the discovery of church growth, much is now being said concerning gifts for the church.

G. Raymond Carlson, assistant general superintendent of the Assemblies of God, states that there are three manifestations of the Spirit (*Spiritual Dynamics* [Springfield, MO: Gospel Publishing House, 1976], p. 97). They are as follows:

1. Gifts of the Spirit.
2. Administrations or gifts of ministry.
3. Operations of the Spirit.

Brother Carlson suggests that these occur in the body of Christ through various members. It should be noted that the word *body* occurs 18 times in 1 Corinthians 12. The word *member* is listed 14 times in the chapter, and the word *gift* is mentioned six times.

A question comes to mind: Are all the gifts supernatural, or are some of them the product of natural talent? It is not difficult to realize that on the highest level, the nine gifts of the Spirit named in 1 Corinthians 12:8-10 are of supernatural origin. These gifts are generally divided into three groups:

1. The mind of God—word of wisdom; word of knowledge; discerning of spirits.
2. The power of God—faith; gifts of healing; miracles.
3. The voice of God—prophecy; tongues; interpretation of tongues.

These gifts of revelation, power, and inspiration we accept as supernatural. Are there other gifts that can help your church grow? I believe that the answer to this question is yes. Brother Carlson suggests:

> In addition to the nine gifts mentioned in 1 Corinthians 12:8-10, there are other gifts. I do make a distinction between the ministry gifts of Ephesians 4 and the manifestations of the Spirit as listed in the Corinthians passage. The ministry gifts are given to the Church by Christ; whereas the nine gifts in 1 Corinthians 12 are given by the Holy Spirit. The ministry gifts are people whom God has called and whom He endows with special abilities. The spiritual gifts of 1 Corinthians 12:8-10 have no relationship to human aptitude but are totally the product of the Holy Spirit. The preacher, teacher, evangelist, and pastor-teacher do not depend solely on a manifestation of God's sovereignty. He must apply himself in preparation and study.

Donald Gee gives information concerning the use and purpose of spiritual gifts. According to Gee (in his book *Concerning Spiritual Gifts*), the growing New Testament Church possessed supernatural features. In the course of their worship, they healed the sick, cast out demons, and raised the dead. They prophesied, spoke in tongues, and, as the Spirit empowered them, participated in signs and wonders. All of these things were the accepted norm in the New Testament Church. The world came to notice this church. The excitement that surrounds the supernatural ministry of the Spirit still draws the world to look at the Church today. This distinct Pentecostal heritage of the Assemblies of God has become a major church growth factor in churches across America and overseas. *The nine gifts of the Spirit, in operation, will cause your church to grow.*

Additional spiritual gifts are mentioned in other New Testament passages. Dr. Anthony Palma gives additional Scripture passages to consider when compiling a list of spiritual gifts:

> And God hath set some in the church, first apostles, secondarily prophets, thirdly teachers, after that miracles, then gifts of healings, helps, governments, diversities of tongues. Are all apostles? are all prophets? are all teachers? are all workers of miracles? have all the gifts of healing? do all speak with tongues? do all interpret? (1 Corinthians 12:28-30).

> Having then gifts differing according to the grace that is given to us, whether prophecy, let us prophesy according to the proportion of faith; or ministry, let us wait on our ministering; or he that teacheth, on teaching; or he that exhorteth, on exhortation: he that giveth, let him do it with simplicity; he that ruleth, with diligence; he that showeth mercy, with cheerfulness (Romans 12:6-8).

> But unto every one of us is given grace according to the measure of the gift of Christ. Wherefore he saith, When he ascended up on high, he led captivity captive, and gave gifts unto men. (Now that he ascended, what is it but that he also descended first into the lower parts of the earth? He that descended is the same also that ascended up far above all heavens, that he might fill all things.) And he gave some, apostles; and some, prophets; and some, evangelists; and some, pastors and teachers (Ephesians 4:7-11).

These passages name a number of spiritual gifts, along with talents and ministries, which are available for the edification of the Body. The list from these passages includes:

word of wisdom	prophecy
word of knowledge	discerning of spirits
faith	tongues
gifts of healing	interpretation of
miracles	tongues

Other church growth ministries include:

apostles	exhortation
prophets	giving
teachers	mercy
helps	ruling
governments	evangelists
ministry	pastor-teachers

I would not want to suggest that this is a complete list of gifts and ministries. It is only a list compiled from Scripture passages given earlier. You will notice that there is some overlapping from one passage to another. In some cases, the passages use different words to name the same gift or ministry.

On the subject of gifts, Dr. Anthony Palma comments: "I'm not sure that Paul ever meant for us to have a complete list of gifts. As I see it, the gifts that he does mention are specific enough that they might suggest other gifts as well."

It is feasible to suggest that some gifts could be given by God to meet specific needs and circumstances. According to Dr. Palma, there are *talents* and there are *gifts*:

There is a difference between a talent and a gift that is given by God for the advancement of God's work. It isn't really a gift until it is used by God for His work. (Statements made by Dr. Palma were taken from an interview taped in September 1980.)

How can we make ourselves available for ministries that relate to church life and growth?

1. Get alone with God. Before we can share with others, we must know ourselves. Ask yourself: "What are my natural abilities? What do I have to

offer to God?" As you take an honest look at yourself, you may be able to seek more intelligently the gift with which you can bless the Body the most.

2. Ask yourself: "How can I best minister to the body of Christ? In what ways will God's kingdom profit most with my contribution?"

3. Ask yourself: "What functions do I now have in the Body?" Before we can move forward, we must know where we are now. An honest appraisal of past activity may prove helpful.

C. Peter Wagner, in his book *Your Spiritual Gifts Can Help Your Church Grow* (Glendale, CA: Gospel Light/Regal Publications, 1979), gives further help to the members of the local church in discovering their place of ministry.

Agree on a Philosophy of Ministry

A philosophy of ministry would include a statement of fundamental truths and further information on what the church expects in the way of ministry. Finding our evangelistic mix will help define our philosophy of ministry. Consider the following:

1. Is our church strong in preaching, music, and so forth? Are we involved in counseling, helping the disenfranchised, or assisting abused families? What are our strengths?

2. We must build within people a growth consciousness. This was alluded to earlier. In some people, it is not something that is developed, but it is a natural awareness—a burning desire to expand our limits at any cost.

3. We must analyze the body. You might ask yourself three sets of questions:
   a. What is my attitude toward myself? What is my personal attitude toward the gospel and the Great Commission? How much of the responsibility of winning the lost do I feel is mine?
   b. What is my attitude toward my church? Is my church friendly? Do I make it friendly? If I were a stranger in my church, would I feel welcome? (When asked for the keys to church growth, a number of churches recently surveyed stated that friendliness to new people was one of the greatest tools.)
   c. What is my attitude toward my community? What are the needs of my community? The attitude with which you view your community will tell you much about the success of your church.

In asking ourselves these questions and looking at members' individual abilities and gifts, we may see where our growth, or lack of it, is coming from. By evaluating our own strengths, growth goals can be enlarged.

4. What are the growth goals of the church? Do we desire to be a family church, a community church? Several years ago, a church that I was acquainted with made the positive decision to readjust their growth goals. Established for many years in a small town, they had maintained their attendance of about 100 adherents for 10 years. By positive action they redesigned their growth goals, moving from a family/community church to a county church reaching many miles in all directions. By

simply enlarging their growth goals and vision, they began reaching people in areas where there was no church. In 3 years, they had doubled their attendance and were continuing to grow. Enlarging our growth goals and vision can be a positive step toward church growth.

5. What are the Biblical convictions of the church? The community must know where we are coming from in light of God's Word. What we believe and how we apply those beliefs to our lives will affect the people with whom we come in contact.

6. How are we using the laity? The next few years will be very important for lay persons involved in the church. Opportunities for ministry, church government, and education will be of primary interest to the lay person. One of the most valuable resources of a church is the experience and expertise of lay persons within the body. The ability to effectively use the laity will greatly enhance the growth of the church.

7. What new units have we established? One healthy sign is to establish at least two new units per year. These could include Sunday school classes, prayer groups, care fellowships, and others.

8. What ministries for growth are available through our members?

9. What growth-restricting obstacles do we face?

10. What are we doing in outreach?

11. What are our denominational distinctives?

A pastor friend related this story recently: "I was pastoring in a Midwestern town that was the home of a major Lutheran university. Our church was growing and, as a young minister, I was excited to see the moving of the Spirit in our congregation.

"One Sunday night as service was beginning, a professor of Biblical studies from the university, along with eight students, walked into our church. My inexperience caused me to freeze at the sight of these folk. I conducted a very formal service, different from what our people were used to.

"After the service, the professor came to me and said, 'I must admit that I was disappointed in this service. I had heard that you folk were different from us.'"

This pastor learned a lesson about denominational distinctives. Be yourself. Don't try to change the church's personality each week to fit the audience.

Initiate a Growth Process

Discovering, developing, and using spiritual ministries can be an end in itself, and it is a good end. In some cases this alone will help a church grow. But church growth is complex and spiritual ministries are only one of many church growth principles. This growth process, including spiritual ministries, comes in part as the church develops a church growth consciousness and church growth eyes (see chapter 2). There are plans and commitments that we need to make to facilitate church growth. Spiritual gifts will fit naturally into the plan for church growth.

Structure for Gifts of Growth

Peter Wagner states in his book on spiritual gifts: "A church needs to be structured administratively for growth." Many forms of church administration unknowingly stifle the ministry of the members. Cumbersome committees and traditions without a scriptural basis have at times slowed down a church's growth rate. The smoothest structure for growth is the one that fully recognizes the leadership position of the pastor and allows him to utilize the various ministries within the church. As a pastor operates with an awareness of spiritual ministries, his example helps others to seek opportunities for service within the body of Christ.

Spiritual ministries are not something that have been dreamed up just to be included in a book. God's Word specifically tells us that spiritual gifts and ministries are for the Church. As we look at ourselves and our function in the Church, we have the right to expect God to work through our lives and in the Church.

Spiritual ministries in proper operation will help your church grow numerically, materially, and spiritually. God wants His children to have active ministries. As we accept His challenge, church growth will occur and lost persons will be found.

5

Defining Church Growth

Church growth is a process of fulfilling the Great Commission through the threefold mission of the Church, believed by the Assemblies of God to include evangelizing the world, the maturing of believers, and worshiping God. Church growth affects all areas of church life with an excitement of becoming all that Christ intended. There is an alertness to new opportunities and an expansion of ministries. The growing church reflects a dynamic faith, a steadfast hope, and a Christlike love. (This definition of church growth was approved by the Executive Presbytery of the Assemblies of God on March 28, 1980).

How do we define church growth in relation to our situation? What does this term mean? Since its inception, the Assemblies of God has been a growth-oriented Fellowship. In its early days, churches were planted across America almost daily. The Assemblies of God assumed leadership worldwide in foreign missionary effort. Sunday schools became a major influence in the community. Assemblies of God churches were *expected* to grow.

Church Growth in the 1970s

With the beginning of the decade of the 1970s, our Fellowship saw a fresh new increase. In the years 1970 to 1975, Assemblies of God Sunday schools grew by 213,186. Many factors contributed to this rapid growth. The bus ministry became the biggest boost to Sunday school growth. Thousands of children attended our churches for the first time through this ministry. The increase in numbers alone spawned new ministries. Children's churches, extended sessions, Kids' Krusades, and other programs were propelled to a place of prominence in the local church.

Additional ministry opportunities ignited a growth explosion early in the decade. Groups of young people met on the west coast to "discover" Jesus Christ. As thousands found a personal relationship with Christ, the "Jesus people" movement was born. New songs, guitars, banners, and marches became symbols of the Jesus movement. Many of the teenagers and young people growing up in the early 1970s married, started their families, and looked for some religious experience akin to that of the Jesus movement. Because of the excitement of our worship services and the freedom of the Spirit of God, many of these people were incorporated into our Fellowship.

Another factor contributing to growth was the electronic church. A new awareness of the Pentecostal message began to flow out from national and international radio and television ministries. Many people caught a glimpse of the spiritual dynamics of the Pentecostal Movement and started looking for a local church that had the same dynamics. A large number of Assemblies of God churches saw growth as a direct result of this media exposure.

The growth patterns and success stories of the early 1970s helped create an appetite for growth across our Fellowship. Pastors, lay persons, and denominational leaders started asking questions: "What is growth? How do we grow? Where is our growth coming from?" Many pastors of growing churches found that they could share exciting testimonies about their churches' growth, but they couldn't give specifics as to how their churches were growing. To fully understand church growth, perhaps we should go back to the beginnings of the modern-day church growth movement.

Origin of the Term "Church Growth"

According to Peter Wagner of Fuller Theological Seminary, church growth was first introduced in the United States by Donald McGavran in 1972. That is not to say, however, that exciting growth did not happen in our Movement before this date. McGavran was a third-generation missionary who spent 30 years preaching on the mission field of India. He noted that some methods common to the traditional church in the United States did not work in foreign lands. He stated that while serving as a missionary on foreign soil, he became aware of God's great plan for the Church. That plan was to not only reach the lost, but also make disciples.

During his years on the mission field, McGavran developed certain concepts and strategies that worked. Looking for a term to describe what he was talking about, he came up with two words that are familiar to all churchmen: *church* and *growth*. This new term, *church growth*, then meant to reach the lost and disciple them. In McGavran's opinion, this is our commission today. McGavran and others soon discovered that the reaching-discipling adventure was not just for the foreign field, but was also a workable plan for American churches.

Church growth principles are reaching unchurched America today. Church growth means that individuals are accepting Christ as Saviour and growing in their faith.

Recently, I visited with Dr. Melvin Hodges, a former Assemblies of God missionary to Latin America and a close friend of Donald McGavran. In that interview he talked of church growth and its effect on church life today. According to Dr. Hodges: "Church growth is the conscious effort to establish the church and the extension of the church through evangelism and teaching." He further stated that every church should grow in two phases: first, the witness of its members; and second, an organizational structure for growth.

Designing Church Structure for Growth

Concerning organizational structure, Dr. Hodges stated the following: "Most church structure is designed for maintenance. All organization must be designed for growth."

Three levels of association form the basic structure for outreach contact. They are worship or celebration, congregational or Sunday school meetings, and small-group or cell meetings. What do these terms mean in relation to growth in the local church? Let's look further.

Worship or Celebration

This may be the first contact that lost persons have with your church. They may be attracted to the singing or the intensity of worship. They may have a deep, personal need. They may admire the pastor or his ability to preach great sermons. How you define your role may help or inhibit growth on this level.

What can you do to create a climate for worship?

1. Be faithful to all services. You may have an opportunity to minister to someone to whom no one else can minister.

2. Participate in congregational singing and prayer. If you are a spectator, others will follow your lead. Active participation encourages others to become involved.

3. Participate in giving. The act of giving and the spirit with which we give does make a difference. A church that gives liberally may expect a full measure of blessing from the Lord.

4. Become involved at altar time. This can be a critical time in the worship service. As believers take the lead in praying, others will follow.

You have a responsible part to play in the celebration service as you define your role in worship.

The Sunday School or Congregational Meeting

Meeting in small groups to study the Word of God, such as in Sunday school, is an excellent example of the congregational meeting. Consider some of the benefits of this type of meeting. Let's look at the adult class for a moment. Class members become better acquainted with each other and with newcomers. They learn to study together, learn more about one another, discuss the Bible and spiritual things, and share prayer requests. This type of contact builds close relationships.

The Small Group or Cell

Dr. Melvin Hodges stated: "The church cell has

been a spin-off of individual initiative that will work if it is a part of a structure." The small group or cell is the third level of association. Small-group worship had its roots in early Assemblies of God growth. These small groups were called "cottage prayer meetings." Small-group worship has had a rebirth in recent years with the growth in the Korean church and the many American success stories.

The following are five directives suggested for small groups (six to eight persons):

1. There should be group worship. This is a major purpose for coming together. Some people feel freer to express themselves in worship in a small, rather than a large, group of people.

I remember one little lady in my church who stood to give a testimony. God had healed some physical problems she had been having. After she stood, she realized she would be talking about a personal, physical problem in front of the whole congregation. So she smiled, blushed, and said, "I have an unspoken testimony!" In a small group of friends, she might have been able to share her testimony and encourage someone else's faith.

2. There should be a study of God's Word. This study need not be as elaborate or detailed as in Sunday school, but it should be on a level of personal sharing.

3. There should be sharing of joys and concerns. One of the great benefits of small groups is that we can minister to one another. Recently, a brother commented: "We had just moved to our town. We did not know anyone. We didn't have any relatives and were quite lonely. Then we were invited to join a prayer group in our church. It has made the difference in our church and home lives."

This family needed to be part of a group of believers. Sharing joys and concerns is one of the benefits of the small group.

4. There should be group prayer. This is something we need. It is a privilege to pray one for another.

5. There should be accountability and responsibility. Everyone needs to be accountable to someone. By open and honest sharing, members of the group can be a blessing to one another.

The ability to share in an open and honest manner with people you care for was brought to my attention in a real way not long ago. With my responsibilities in the national Sunday School Department, I traveled thousands of miles each year. It was sometimes necessary for me to be away from home for weeks at a time. This meant ministering in a different church almost every weekend. I met on a monthly basis with a group of men from Springfield for prayer and fellowship. We shared needs and fellowship and prayed together. This prayer meeting was a blessing to me personally.

After having been on the road for some time, spending many hours in airports, and having a heavy workload, I went to a prayer meeting. One of the brothers in the group commented to me, "Mike, you're tired." I quickly agreed that I was very tired of airports, cafeterias, and motel rooms. He said, "With all that you've been doing, you haven't had time for your daily devotions, have you?"

In one sense he was correct. I had been so involved in preaching, teaching, and ministering, that my private devotions had slipped a little. Now I should say at this point that I wasn't doing anything I shouldn't have been doing; I was just tired. This brother's concern touched my heart. If we had not been sharing close fellowship, and if I weren't convinced that he was concerned for me as a brother in Christ, I would have advised him to back off. But he was showing genuine Christian love. From then on it became a priority for me to spend time in prayer, even while staying in a motel room. I did not want to disappoint myself or this concerned brother.

We are responsible to one another. Responsibility for others will consistently draw members closer to each other in Christ.

The Mission of the Church

As we further define church growth, let's look at our mission. Where do you fit in the overall mission of the Church?

Evangelizing the World

You will not be able to reach the whole world, but by starting where you are now, you can help fan the flame of evangelism around the world. Individual initiative multiplies itself as one person reaches out to another in an endless cycle.

Evangelism happens many times in "people webs." Take my friend David, for instance. David is a Christian. He lives in Kansas City, Missouri, and works in a steel mill. Since Dave is like most of us, he has friends at work and at other places. By his personal life and verbal testimony he was able to win two friends at work to Christ. As their lives were changed, they started a "people web." Sam, one of those new converts, told a friend of his about the Lord. This friend shared his new faith with his wife, who told her neighbor. This people web is an important step in evangelizing our world.

The Institute for American Church Growth estimates that the average Christian has a number of contacts with people who are not Christians. This may vary depending on the length of time since conversion. As we touch people, who in turn touch others, we are beginning New Testament evangelism.

The Maturing of Believers

A young woman in a San Francisco suburb recently gave birth to an 8 pound 10 ounce baby boy. According to a newspaper source, she had always wanted a baby. The boy was healthy in every way. Four days after his birth, however, he was found in a phone booth by a police officer who was making his rounds. The baby later died at the hospital. How horrible! The world, as well as the Church, is shocked at such happenings.

Could similar accusations be made against the Church? Never! And yet, in some ways, the Church may be responsible for the spiritual death of its members. We do have a responsibility to new converts. The maturing of believers is a major task of the Church. Deuteronomy 31:12, 13 gives direction to the Children of Israel and points out their responsibility to others:

> Gather the people together, men, and women, and children, and thy stranger that is within thy gates, that they may hear, and that they may learn, and fear the LORD your God, and observe to do all the words of this law: and that their children, which have not known any thing, may hear, and learn to fear the LORD your God, as long as ye live in the land.

God's promise to the Children of Israel was that if they would be strong and of good courage He would bring them and their children into the Promised Land. This speaks of maturity and growth.

The national Sunday School Department of the Assemblies of God recently stated its reason for being. It is similar to this Scripture passage—to reach, teach, win, mature, and train lost persons. The mission of the Church is to bring men, women, and children to a meaningful place in Christ as they grow and mature in God's Word.

Worshiping God

We have already talked about our opportunities in worship. We have shared the need to create a climate for the worship experience. It should be said at this point that there are many forms of worship. What may be appropriate in some circles, may not be in others. Different people react differently to the moving of God's Spirit. I have been made more aware of this recently through extensive travel across America. It is exciting to observe so many different kinds of worship, and yet there are similarities. People who are worshiping God have two things in common: their love for the Lord and their desire to please Him. As we keep this in mind, we will fulfill the true mission of the Church.

Defining church growth is not an easy task. The definition will encompass different ingredients from place to place. As we maintain a scriptural pattern for growth and seek to fulfill our mission, our personal church growth definition will come into focus.

6

Understanding Today's Opportunities

The mission of the church for these last decades of the 20th century has not changed. Our primary task is still to "take the gospel to every creature." The message of the church cannot change. It is solidly based on God's Word and is one of those fixed entities that remains dependable regardless of the circumstances of the age. (Thomas F. Zimmerman, general superintendent of the Assemblies of God. This quotation is from a speech given on August 10, 1980 in Springfield, Missouri.)

The Church and the world are standing at one of the greatest crossroads in the history of mankind. For the world, the opportunity to communicate worldwide has never been greater. Scientific, economic, social, and medical discoveries are changing our life-styles. The progression of man, in his own opinion, will either bring him lasting peace or the total destruction of the world. Mankind is facing a crisis.

The Church, too, is standing at a critical crossroads. There are greater opportunities, more openness, and more genuine ministry taking place now than at any other time in the history of the Church. The individual church that understands its place of ministry and can define its personal mission during these exciting and difficult days will undoubtedly see great church growth during the decade.

We have already been made aware of the newly adopted definition of church growth, but what about the mission of the individual church? Let's take a closer look.

It has been said that the Church is a hospital that ministers to human needs. One of the most beautiful and tragic scenes painted in the Bible is found in John 5. John tells of the man lying by the pool of Bethesda. We are made aware of an intense struggle. According to the Bible, the man had been ill for 38 years. At certain seasons, an angel came to stir the water and whoever got into the pool first received healing. Can you imagine the competition as folks struggled for position? Just to be first into the water!

One day Jesus came on the scene and inquired of the man about his condition. Verses 7-9 tell us:

> The impotent man answered him, Sir, I have no man, when the water is troubled, to put me into the pool: but while I am coming, another steppeth down before me. Jesus saith unto him, Rise, take up thy bed, and walk. And immediately the man was made whole, and took up his bed, and walked.

Jesus became the Man on the scene to bring life back to this pitiful man.

The Church is a healing station today. There are scores and scores of people in the ministry area of your church waiting for someone to step in and help them. Sometimes even the Church becomes too busy to become involved. One of the great opportunities of the Church today is to care.

My wife and I know the effects of a caring church on our lives. We were pastoring a little church in the central part of the state of Iowa. Even though it had grown some, it was still quite small. Winter in Iowa can be a real experience, and April 1972 was no exception. A late winter snow paralyzed the town where we pastored.

I remember being awakened from a deep sleep one night during that snowstorm. Our 1-year-old daughter was crying. We went into her bedroom and found her lying in her bed in a pool of her own blood. Her face looked as if it had been cut many times. We learned later that morning that our daughter had been attacked by a rabid rat. The animal had sought shelter from the cold and had come into our small home through the plumbing. Jenny had been bitten five times in the face. We could not tell anyone how we felt as the doctor told us there was no cure for rabies and our child might eventually die.

It was during this time, while our daughter was in critical condition in and out of the hospital, that we learned that the church is a hospital of sorts. What a privilege it was to come from a place of uncertainty where there seemed to be no hope to that small church where believers offered encouragement and prayers. We learned that the prayer of faith saves the sick and it is God's will to heal. The doctor summed it up best when he said: "I don't understand prayer, but you and your church must have something going for you."

Today, Jenny is a healthy young lady without one scar from her ordeal!

I am convinced that the local church is a hospital whose purpose is to touch, heal, and change lives. Healing takes many forms. It touches the body, mind, and spirit of man. The Church must touch people at the level of their need.

Consider these directives of our mission:

To Reach the Lost

The Pentecostal church has a great advantage in reaching the lost today. Spreading the gospel is predominant in our concern. Many new and innovative methods are being used, but the message does not change.

The Church Is Reaching Out Through Individual Witnessing

Folks are sharing their faith as never before. Classes on personal evangelism, successful lay leadership, and the anointing of the Holy Spirit, have sent thousands out with the desire to witness. It has been noted that the most winnable people are relatives and friends: individuals reaching individuals.

The concept of "people webs"—touching those people with whom we have established credibility—is a proven method of evangelism. I interviewed a pastor of an east coast church not long ago. He stated that many souls had been saved recently in his church. When asked how this was being accomplished, he replied: "It's happening in homes. Friends are sharing their faith with friends and others." Personal evangelism (one-on-one contact) is still the greatest outreach tool of the Church today.

The Church Is Reaching Out With the Pentecostal Distinctive

Many still do not understand speaking in tongues, but there is genuine interest in the Holy Spirit today. Thousands of charismatics are flocking to the Assemblies of God in an effort to find the "gift." As churches are sensitive to this hunger for the charismatic experience, many fringe people will be brought into the church.

The Church Is Reaching Out Through the Electronic Media

The electronic church is an addition to ministry in the local church. According to Dan Betzer, *Revivaltime* evangelist, the electronic church is not in competition with local ministries. Brother Betzer stated: "More people are becoming aware of their need for Christ through this medium than any other." As unchurched people become aware of the excitement of Pentecostal worship, they seek out a congregation with like values. It is up to us to provide the same excitement and desire. While ministries will vary from church to church, this same excitement and desire can be manifested in our services and used to reach people.

The Growing Church and Christian Education

If it is true that adults are flocking back to the classroom, Christian education is a great growth opportunity today. Both young people and adults need Christian education. They need doctrinal stability for further learning. Fellowship, instruction in the value of church membership, and stewardship will also come through the Christian education process.

Jesus said to go and teach. It has been said: "Cook a fish for a little boy's breakfast and he will be filled up; but teach him to fish and he will never go hungry." As we are involved in education and training, the Church is supplying spiritual food for generations to come.

The Growing Church Has a Commitment to the Family

Something should be said about the quality of life. At times it seems that the church and family are in competition. The prize is time. Too often in the name of growth we rob the family of time in order to make a program work. A friend who is an Assemblies of God minister on the east coast related the following story.

In 1971 he was called to pastor a certain assembly. It had once been a great church. Several of its pastors had become district leaders. However, at that time, the congregation was discouraged and down to only 19 members. The pastor was 27 years old and overflowing with determination. The first 4 years were painful, but the heart and foundation of the assembly stood firm. The prayers and faithfulness of its former great pastors began to produce fruit. People began to get saved. Believers experienced healings and dynamic encounters with the Lord. It was harvesttime.

As growth began to occur, the pastor found himself enjoying the increased hours of labor. His wife started to drop hints about how many hours he was putting into the church. He felt tension building between them. He tried to assure her that his schedule would get back to normal in "just a little while."

He was excited. The church was on the move. They began to look for land, for they knew building was inevitable. He was in the office for hours on end.

His counseling load averaged 20 to 25 hours each week. Fifteen hours a week went into the radio program. To keep up with the schedule meant arriving at the office early and returning home late. Many days he did not see his three children except when he peeked in on them as they slept, before he dropped into bed, exhausted. Several times he came home to find his wife weeping in depression. He began to feel the tension. The children started to rebel against going to church. Still he worked, promising himself just a little longer and then everything would be okay.

Then it happened. He finally gave in to his wife's begging to take a day off. They decided to visit friends who pastored in another community. The 1-hour trip took almost 3 hours!

My friend made the following statement: "I knew the way perfectly. We had been there many times, but on this day I began to come apart. I was disoriented, driving up and down the same highway, unable to remember which way was right. Finally I pulled off the road and began to shake and weep. When we finally arrived, my wife, realizing what was happening, made me go right to bed. I slept almost 18 hours. How I got through that Sunday's services, only God knows.

"On Monday, I called my secretary and told her to cancel all my appointments that day. I would not be coming into the office. I sat at the kitchen table across from my wife. We wrote down what my schedule had been for the past 6 months. It revealed that I had averaged almost 100 hours a week in actual working time. *No* time—much less quality time—had been spent with her or my children.

"If I am totally honest, I must tell you that my

devotional time with God was sadly neglected. We were strictly business partners. It was time for a change."

Together they laid out the following new schedule of priorities: (1) God and private devotional time for feeding on His Word; (2) Wife—time alone with no interruptions; (3) Children—quality time with the family together and special time alone with each child; (4) Vocation—pastoral duties. (A former associate of Rev. Jerry Falwell, Rev. Larry Troy, states: "The pastor working more than 60 hours a week is either robbing God or his family, or both."); (5) Ministry—true ministry does not take place until it has passed through this filtering system. Only then is it pure ministry.

This pastor states: "In 3 short weeks our family experienced miraculous healing. Our ministry began to flow out of 'what we were,' instead of 'what we did.' The growth that developed at that point made the first stage look small. His yoke truly is easy when we do it His way. When we allow the Church to be the Church that Christ ordained instead of the Church modified by man's concepts, she will heal and give life to the family; she will promote and nurture the family; she will continually and unfailingly lead the family into maturity and ministry that will magnify and model the Church's true message."

It needs to be reemphasized that the church and family are not in competition. Family ministries, marriage-enrichment seminars, singles' and seniors' ministries, all contribute to the growth of the body. As we by design increase the quality of family life in relation to the church, we are enhancing the long-range growth goals of workers and of the Church.

A young minister asked me recently: "After God, what should be the most important? The church or my family?" There might have been a time when I would have been expected to say the church. Not so today. We will never be the pastors, teachers, leaders, or lay persons we should be, if we are not first committed to our families. As our churches provide family ministry and give time back to our church families, we will grow.

The Growing Church Has Responsibility for Training

We must reproduce ourselves. New converts will be ineffective without training, helps, and patterns to follow. Training, Christian living, and evangelism are vital. There is a church growth term called *ingrowth*. Ingrowth means we only look inward to ourselves. Training must be structured *outward*. The church that practices ingrowth will die in two generations.

Consider with me some opportunities for the 1980s. Not all methods will work in every situation. We must allow the Holy Spirit to direct us to the growth opportunities of our situation.

Adult Elective Programs

Many church families are finding that elective scheduling speaks to specific needs of the local body. Adult electives may be placed alongside regular education classes. These electives could involve college-level classes, doctrine, prophecy, practical helps, and others. Many folk in the community will respond to classes that speak directly to their needs.

Flexibility in Scheduling

Work and travel patterns, city and rural differences, energy needs, weather problems, and other factors may cause the church to become more flexible in its scheduling during this decade. It may become necessary to break with tradition in scheduling.

First Assembly in Grand Forks, North Dakota, holds services on Saturday as well as on Sunday. The church is located near a military base. This fact, combined with a lack of space, caused them to begin having 2 days of services. It has worked well in their situation. Many churches now have two Sunday morning services. This may be for convenience, but it's also because of space requirements. With higher interest rates, and building and land costs escalating, we may see more congregations going to dual services.

A church in a southwest metropolitan area showed flexibility in Sunday scheduling. They had Sunday school and morning worship at the usual time. After dinner on the grounds, or a trip to a nearby restaurant, their Sunday evening service took place at 3:00 in the afternoon. The reason for this early service stemmed from the energy crisis in their area and the fact that many of their members were scattered all over the city. Their innovative scheduling showed concern for the needs of their people.

Family Mass Transit

This may also be called bus ministry. It is still a viable ministry today. As gasoline becomes more costly and more families become involved in the worship experience, this may be a means of reaching both children and adults.

Cable Television

Some congregations are already experimenting with a cable television ministry, both in evangelism and in teaching. With the majority of American homes having access to cable television during the 1980s, this opportunity should not be ignored.

Home Groups

Small-group worship is on the increase in the American church. If small-group worship is done properly and for the right reasons it will contribute to the growth of the entire body.

National and Regional Training Conferences

In recent years, the Council on Evangelism, the Church Growth Convention, conferences on the Holy Spirit, and marriage and family enrichment conferences have brought high-level training to our Fellowship. Quality meetings of this nature will continue to offer helps in growth.

There are many opportunities available relating to growth during the 1980s. Men of God who are involved in growing churches will be the first to say, "Investigate, study, pray, learn from others, and then adapt the methods to the needs of your community." Our mission has not changed. The church is a hospital to heal the needs of lost people.

As we understand our growth opportunities, apply growth principles, and anticipate God's increase, our churches will grow.

7

What Kind of Church Is This?

Is it a rural or city church? An upper-middle class or a lower income congregation? It is important to know the kind of church your congregation is.

Peter Wagner, church growth strategist, recently made this observation concerning the Assemblies of God: "There are basically two kinds of [Assemblies of God] churches: the front-door church, and the side-door church."

The Front-door or Side-door Church

If you, as an adult, have grown up in an Assemblies of God Sunday school, you probably attended a "side-door church" during your early years. In the side-door church, new people usually have their first contact with the church through the Sunday school, youth meetings, or other group meetings. In the 1950s and early 1960s, the pastor of the side-door church was concerned because he never had quite as many people stay for the worship service as came to the Sunday school. The side-door church met the community needs and brought growth to the Sunday school.

Innovative growth trends and new opportunities in the late 1960s and 1970s brought many churches to "front-door" status. Simply stated, the front-door church means that new people have their first contact with the church through the worship or celebration service. They are saved, or incorporated into the worship body, and then drawn to groups such as the Sunday school, men's ministries, the youth group, etc.

There are several reasons for this shift from side-door to front-door status.

The Charismatic Renewal

Thousands upon thousands of nominal Christians heard the Pentecostal message for the first time during the late 1960s. Charismatic Catholics, students on college campuses, and businessmen were exposed to Pentecost. As hunger for this experience grew, many people looked to the Assemblies of God for leadership. These folk naturally came in the front door to the worship service. Charismatics are becoming established today in the local church.

The Electronic Church

We have already spoken of the electronic church, but it has been and still is a factor in front-door church growth. National, international, and even local radio and television programs have given a taste of the Pentecostal experience to the American public. When they have gone looking for this experience, they have found it in the front-door worship service.

Jesus People

Front-door church growth came from an unexpected source. Young people, disenchanted by the government and by business, started looking for something else. They took to the streets, marching and singing about Jesus. I interviewed a "Jesus people" person recently. He made the following observation: "We took to the streets, marching and singing and having a great time with Jesus. Some of us really got saved. After a time we acquired families and jobs and, in the process, became separated from the youthful Jesus movement. I was looking for the same feeling we had in the Jesus people meetings. I found it in the Assemblies of God church."

The Jesus people movement did not affect church growth in all geographic areas, but particularly on the west coast and in the southeast.

There are other factors too numerous to mention that caused some churches to begin ministering through the front door. It does not matter whether a church is a front-door or side-door ministry, as long as they know which one they are.

Community Analysis

If we are to become a growing church in the community, it is necessary to know what kind of church we are and to be aware of specific needs in our community.

Community analysis, as a scientific approach to church growth, can help establish goals and give direction. What are the criteria for community analysis? Four types of analysis that can be used to effectively determine opportunities of church growth in your community include: geographic, sociological, demographic, and religious. We will look at these four methods of evaluation, suggest tools that can be used, and discuss the effects of evaluation on the church.

Several items should be considered in a geographic analysis of the community. Consider the following list:

1. Identify the boundaries of your ministry area. If your church is located in a large city, you may wish to establish a perimeter within an 8- to 10-mile radius of your church. (Some churches think in terms of minutes, not miles.) If your church is located in a small town or rural setting, your ministry area may include city or county limits or a natural geographic boundary, such as a river, a mountain range, etc.

We must not be limited by these areas, but establish them as a plan of action to provide direction for consistent church growth.

2. Determine what other churches are in your ministry area. It would be helpful to chart their location on a map. Are other churches already meeting the needs of the people you are trying to reach? Are there areas where no one is involved in ministry?

3. What special housing projects or institutions are located in your ministry area? Schools, hospitals, colleges, retirement villages, military installations, or a large apartment complex may provide some insight into the ministry needed. By contacting the city planning commission, you might be able to determine what new projects are on the drawing board.

4. Define a primary and secondary area of outreach. Many churches are frustrated as they spread themselves too thin in outreach. Others waste effort, time, and money in overlapping

ministries. Duplicity seldom pays dividends. Your primary area of outreach may be determined by accessibility to the church, or by the number of members living in a certain area. It will also be related to need. Primary interest could be determined by a growing bedridden community or a rapidly expanding college.

The primary area of concern in most cases will be a homogeneous grouping. A homogeneous group is made up of people with common goals, common interests, and in many cases a common economic background. Members of a homogeneous group usually live in much the same type of neighborhood. Communications flow easily among the people in the group. These same people, when brought into the church, will adapt quickly, feel comfortable, and respond to the ministry with ease. The greatest church growth success will occur in the primary-interest homogeneous group.

Secondary areas of concern may be determined by current events and happenings. They could include ministry in a prison or to a group of transient workers. With the secondary ministry group, the church may have to adapt itself to different surroundings.

Ministry to primary and secondary areas of concern, when charted on a geographic basis, may be done in phases, depending on need and opportunity. This allows the church to work at its own speed and ability. It also provides for a consistent method of outreach.

Calvin Durham, former Sunday school director of the North Texas District of the Assemblies of God, suggested answering the following when conducting a community analysis:

1. Are there areas of concern within our city that have been overlooked by all the churches?

2. How can we better minister to newcomers within our area?

3. Have we overlooked any class or racial group?

4. What can we do to fill open gaps on the map?

A map displayed prominently and colored pins or gummed labels marking the progress of the church's outreach would be an inspiration to church members. Some agencies that may be helpful when doing a geographic analysis would include: the city planning department; the regional council of government; utility companies; county planning agencies (for example: The United Way Planning and Research Division); the county atlas and plat map; the United States Department of Commerce, Census Bureau, Washington, D.C. 20402.

Sociological Analysis

Looking from a sociological perspective, Paul Benjamin states: "Social groups make up the building blocks of any society." If we are to effectively minister to the community, it is necessary to understand the various types of people and their needs.

Maslow's Hierarchy of Human Needs lists five basic needs of the individual. The list includes physical, security, social, self-respect, and achievement needs. We will add one additional need to the list—spiritual need.

1. *Physical need*—People are hurting and looking for someone who can alleviate the pain. We must realize that the Church will never touch every individual at the level of his/her physical need. By yield-

ing to the Spirit's directive, however, many can be touched. As we seek to understand and minister to needs, it may mean praying the prayer of faith for the sick or being a "good Samaritan" in a time of hardship. Touching people at their physical need may allow us to move to the next level of human need.

2. *Security need*—The New Testament speaks of terrible days when men's hearts will fail them for fear. The Bible also talks about perilous times to come. If we believe and understand the Scriptures, it is not hard to realize man's need for security. Will the money market fail? What about Arab oil? Will the United States face famine or war? There are people in your community who are terrified of this world and what the future will bring. We must learn how to reach them with the message of peace.

3. *Social need*—Many individuals are looking for acceptance. Social relations or fellowship (see chapter 3) will be an important part of an individual's relationship.

4. *Self-respect need*—Not long ago, I spoke with a professional Christian counselor on the subject of self-respect. She stated that one of the biggest problems facing the average American today is a bad self-image. Self-worth is essential to good health. As the Church understands this special need and provides a means of gaining self-respect, the individual and the Church will mature.

5. *Achievement need*—Everyone works at a different pace. As we seek to minister to the individual, it is important to allow room and time for personal achievement. Meeting this need may mean a

pastor encouraging members to find their ministry or a teacher challenging his class to explore the Bible for themselves. A proper sense of well-being comes as this need is met.

6. *Spiritual need*—This must be added to the list of needs. We are spiritual persons. The church must determine what spiritual needs are present in the community. By touching the other needs mentioned earlier, the church can then minister to the primary, spiritual need.

What religious groups are in your ministry area? Do they reflect the thinking of the majority in the community? Is there an ethnic or racial majority or minority? What political and economic strengths may be found? Is there a social or economic class structure in the community?

Dr. Benjamin states that economics are at "the heart of the sociological pattern of a community." A person's self-image may be affected by the thickness of his pocketbook. For this reason, some folk (on both ends of the economic scale) might be less receptive to the gospel than others. We must reach out to all social levels. However, the most receptive people will probably be those with whom we have commonalties (see the earlier discussion on the homogeneous group).

Demographic Analysis

Demography is a statistical study of human populations. It deals with population size and density, mobility patterns, and the characteristics and patterns of certain age-groups. A demographic analysis can give specific direction to the church that is embarking on an outreach program.

A friend recently used a demographic analysis to gain insight into a new ministry. He was concerned about ministering to single persons in his church, but he wondered if this was a real need or a temporary, local situation. Through reading he learned that, according to a major news source, every fifth house in America houses a single person (never-married, divorced, or widowed). He determined from this information that it was time to form not only a singles' ministry, but also a ministry to senior citizens. He became aware of needs through studying population, age, sex, and marital-status data.

Information of this nature may save your church time, effort, and expense as you look for the most meaningful opportunity of service. A demographic analysis will help the church become aware of groups and subgroups. For example, there are the obvious divisions of male and female. Beyond this, adults fall into various age strata—young, middle, and older groups—each having its own needs. There are married and unmarried adults; those with children and those without children. Also to be considered are the divorced and the widowed. One can easily see a multitude of needs and ministries to meet these needs that can be offered by the local church.

A demographic analysis might help determine specific needs and long-range goals for outreach.

Religious Analysis

In completing a community analysis, we must include a religious analysis. Americans are more aware of the effect of the church on their lives, than perhaps any other nation. Religious leaders have given input to the economic, social, and political fortunes of the world.

Some questions to ask ourselves are: "What are our denominational distinctives? Are we a soul-winning church? Is our strength education or evangelism? Are we effective in music ministry? Are we known for outstanding preaching?"

We dare not change the message God has given us. However, after conducting a community analysis, we may wish to take a fresh new look at methods. Most congregations really do care about reaching the lost. Some are hindered because they do not know how to reach people. They have been unable to learn the needs of the people they are trying to reach.

A community analysis will not solve all the problems facing a growing church, but it will provide information and insight as the church seeks to fulfill God's plan.

8

Trends in Church Growth

Churches across America are growing; from Bellevue, Nebraska, to Galliano, Louisiana. A new church is growing in Buffalo, New York. First Assembly in Athens, Ohio, has tripled in 4 years. From Northern Minnesota to Los Angeles, church growth is igniting a spark of evangelism. The future of the church looks bright. The 1980s have been declared by men across the nation as the "Decade of Church Growth."

While realizing that just saying this doesn't make it happen, there is a feeling of excitement and expectancy among believers. Church growth is not limited to one geographic area of the nation. At one time churches in the Bible Belt (Midwest) were expected to grow; now churches in every corner of the United States are experiencing explosive growth. The most recent area to see dynamic church growth is the Northeast. Heavy in population, but small in the number of churches, the Northeast is seeing a great revival today.

There are common bonds and individual triumphs that are definite trends in church growth. We will look at some of these trends in the following pages.

Leadership

The role of the leader will be discussed in a later

chapter, but it is necessary to mention here that the leader is God's spokesman. In a recent survey of the 300 fastest-growing churches in America, the question was asked: "What role does the leader play in the overall growth picture of the church?" A large majority responded by saying that leadership is essential to church growth.

It seems apparent that strong leadership, motivating the lay person, will cause the church to grow. A wise pastor knows that he cannot do all the work himself. But in extending himself through his members, much will be accomplished.

In conversation with a pastor recently, the subject of leadership came up. The pastor stated, "I never seem to have time to get everything done!" He went on to say, "I know I should delegate work to others. My problem is I just can't give up my work to other people."

This may be a problem that is common to many. The leader must be willing to empty himself of things such as pride and busywork, to allow others the opportunity of ministry. As the leader empties himself and allows others to grow, his example could lead to great personal and church-wide growth.

Evangelism

Churches that are growing are evangelistic in nature. They may have many different characteristics, but they will maintain the primary purpose of reaching the lost.

People's Church (Assemblies of God) in Arnold, Missouri, has maintained an evangelistic thrust in their community through a bus ministry. Reaching over 700 children and adults each week, their stated purpose is: "Not just bus riders, but souls won to Christ." This commitment pays big dividends.

In a recent *Pentecostal Evangel* article, titled "Kim White Misses Camp," Pastor Kenneth Brown told of a 9-year-old girl named Kim White who made her first trip to church on a Sunday school bus. Coming from a broken home, this little girl was thrilled to know somebody cared for her. She got on the bus one Sunday morning after service with tears in her eyes. She had just accepted Jesus into her life. She was so excited that she would be able to take her newfound Friend to camp. But she never made it to camp. Kim, her little sister, and her mother died in an apartment fire in St. Louis, Missouri, 2 weeks before camp time. According to Brother Brown, bus ministry evangelism pays.

Pastor Ken File of Bethel Assembly of God, in Rock Island, Illinois, is using another form of evangelistic outreach. Prime-time television specials at Christmas, Easter, summertime, and Thanksgiving have provided opportunities to reach people. Using gifted members of the church in testimony, music, drama, and production, this evangelistic outreach has already won many entire families to the Lord. Phone counselors are stationed at the church during and after the television special. Many have been saved and incorporated into the Body through this outreach program.

A church in North Dakota recently instituted a "We Care" program for their community. They were looking for a way to say to the community, "We care about your spiritual condition, but also about other areas of your life." They held classes for young parents on child care and discipline. Other classes included Christian weight watchers for interested persons, and various other opportunities for both men and women. This program has led to a one-on-one witnessing adventure with new prospects. Many have found the Lord through this outreach program.

There are other examples of evangelistic outreach that are interesting and varied in their approach. What comes through from each program is the church's burning desire to reach the lost. Methods will vary from place to place, but the message and the reason for involvement are the same.

Vision

The Bible says in Proverbs 29:18: "Where there is no vision, the people perish."

It is true that when the leadership and the congregation have vision, the body will flourish. We accept it as fact that most congregations do have a spiritual vision. It is not hard to imagine lost souls reaching out to you.

But practical vision is also needed. The church that works as if it expects the Lord to come at any moment, but looks ahead 10 to 15 years or longer, will be in a growth trend. Note the following suggestions:

1. *Write your goals down.* If goals are not concrete enough to be put on paper, you may not know when you have reached them.

2. *Put yourself on a time schedule.* Decide which things should be done this week, this year. Ask the question: "Where should we be in 5 years? in 10 years?"

3. *Evaluate your program.* Ask the question: "Have we accomplished before God our goals or our reason for being?"

By using scientific methods and honest evaluation, we can note where we are today and where we will be in the future. Implementing a spiritual and practical vision is a growth trend of the 1980s.

Consistency

Consistency in the attitudes and actions of a pastor or lay leader is desirable. Another word for consistency is predictability. When people can anticipate how you will react to a situation, they will be more apt to share needs, problems, and insights. Predictability comes from a day-to-day working relationship with people.

The church growth trend, as it relates to a pastor, is to establish long tenure. Moving to a "greener pasture" every year or so does not give a pastor time to build relationships. Fast-growing churches and large churches tend to find a good pastor and keep him. Lay persons in a growing church will also benefit from consistency in their dealings with the pastor and other church leaders.

Flexibility (The Ability to Change)

A definite trend in the 1980s is flexibility. The message does not change. Methods, however, may be adapted to meet specific situations and circumstances. An outstanding trend of the growing church today is the ability to adapt to a place or situation while keeping the close bond of fellowship with the Assemblies of God intact. It is interesting to see so many different kinds of Assemblies of God churches using varied and unique methods to grow, while maintaining their relationship with our Fellowship.

George Edgerly made an interesting observation recently:

> A principle has been observed in franchise marketing. Up to 5,000 units, uniformity is prized. After 5,000 units, distinctiveness is valued. McDonald's and Kentucky Fried Chicken are prime examples. Once every restaurant was built from identical plans. While this is no longer true, their logos still identify them as the place where you can "get a break today," and "feel good about a meal." We do not need every congregation stamped out of the same mold, but we do need to maintain our mutual identification. (George Edgerly made this statement at a workshop on church growth in Alexandria, Virginia, in March 1977).

Flexibility, knowing what to change and when to change, can contribute to growth in the local church.

Quality in Ministry

It is not enough to get folk out to church. We must have spiritual food prepared when they arrive. This is one reason some churches that showed rapid growth in the 1970s declined just as quickly near the end of the decade.

Quality ministry will touch the Christian education area. How we recruit and train our teachers speaks to the quality of ministry. The tools we provide and the motivation we give will be factors in the overall quality.

Quality in ministry will affect the worship service, both on the pastoral level and in the participation of lay persons.

Ted Engstrom, speaking at a church growth convention, made this statement: "God never allows the good to be the enemy of the best." The trend in growing churches today is to provide the best services possible. Quality education, well-prepared music programs, and exciting and spiritual worship experiences, all contribute to excellence.

Adult Emphasis

A new trend in church growth is increased interest in ministry to adults. While in the past energy has been channeled to other areas, the church and the world are now aware of adult trends. According to the U.S. Department of Commerce, population statistics will shift drastically in favor of the middle and senior adult in the 1980s. Consider the following Department of Commerce projections:

Under age 20—up 2.1%
Ages 20-29—down 4.3%
Ages 30-39—up 28.5%
Ages 40-49—up 37.4%
Ages 50-64—down 2%
Ages 65 and over—up 19.6%

With the age-mix change, the church that recognizes the potential of adult ministries will be a growing church. The new adult majority will possess tremendous political, economic, and social clout. The secular world recognizes this and is taking steps to reach the adult market. Advertising is a good gauge of adult power. A decade ago, advertising was directed to the youth population. Today the market is the middle adult. The church must provide helps, fulfillment, and a new challenge to the adult. Truly this is an adult world.

Children's Ministries

With all the interest in adult ministries, we must not neglect children's ministries. A church that fails to reach its children will die.

One congregation in the western central part of the United States 10 years ago was a strong, healthy church. They were financially secure, had a large missionary budget, and from every indication, were an aggressive, growing church. While visiting that church a few years ago, I noticed there were few children in the congregation. The congregation was comprised largely of middle and senior adults. For some reason they were not taking steps to reach the children. In just one decade, without new life coming into the church, it started to die. Today it is near extinction. An Old Testament verse comes to mind: "Give me children, or else I die" (Genesis 30:1).

Trends in children's ministry include the new "2-2-2 program." This is a program that breaks the children into groups according to grades: first and second graders (primaries), third and fourth graders (middlers), and fifth and sixth graders (juniors). This curriculum gives more personalized instruction at the various age-levels and also provides opportunities for learning activities.

Another trend in children's ministries is to have men working in the younger classes. Some children that come to your church may be from single-parent homes. They may not have a male role model. Christian men in the classroom will make a lasting impression on young lives.

Extended sessions are being used in growing churches. The extended session allows continuity in a 2½- to 3-hour Sunday morning time span. It provides better care for larger numbers of children. (There is also a trend toward having larger classes and team teachers.)

Alternating Workers

The popularity of the substitute teacher concept is dwindling. Many growing churches have regularly assigned teacher's aides in the classroom. This allows the alternate teacher to become familiar with the children and with methods of classroom instruction. The alternate teaches one Sunday a month; giving the teacher a rest. This may increase the "teaching life" of the teacher.

Parent-Teacher Conference

Growing churches are adapting this idea from secular education. Meetings between the teacher and the parents can prove meaningful to both parties. Undetected observation by parents of their children may give insight into their children's needs and accomplishments.

Children's ministries are not limited to Sunday morning. Auxiliary groups such as Royal Rangers and Missionettes leave a lasting imprint on young lives. The growing church must be willing to invest in young lives.

Family Life Ministry

A major growth trend in the 1980s will be family life ministry. This area of concern may include marriage enrichment, Christian fathering, parent-child relationships, singles' and senior adults' ministries. We must also provide help and instruction for our children and young people in the Biblical concepts of family, home, marriage, and human sexuality.

The church and the family are not in competition. We must make room for quality family time in the home. Churches are beginning to realize this and are keeping certain evenings of each week free from any activity.

Family life ministry will touch every area of church life. When properly administered, it will enrich the quality of family life.

An excellent resource book to use in introducing family life ministry is: *The Church and Family—A Teaching Team*, by J. D. Middlebrook and Larry Summers (Springfield, MO: Gospel Publishing House, 1980). As the church and the family work together, both will benefit.

Church growth is here to stay. Trends point to a renewed commitment to the church and the lost. Trends may give direction, but you must find God's perfect plan for your situation. There is a growth plan for your church.

9

Removing the Obstacles

While on a church growth tour of the northeastern United States recently, the party I was with drove by a church that had real problems. This church was beautiful, freshly painted, and had a steeple and a church bell. The lawn was well cared for and even the shrubs had been trimmed. But, the church had an attitude problem. The congregation may not have realized it, but the community did. There was a large sign in front of the church that said, "Everyone Welcome." However, under those friendly words were these: "Parking for members only." Now how could one possibly feel welcome if he could not park his car there? Perhaps they did not mean to say this, but the message the community received was: "We are not a friendly church."

Certain opportunities, if we choose to make use of them, will help the church grow. Other actions, intentional or unintentional, may hinder the growth of the local church. Let us consider some hindrances to church growth.

Facilities

When we think of problems affecting the growth of the local church, facilities, more often than not, become the topic of conversation. Right or wrong, facilities get blamed when the church doesn't grow.

Not long ago, I overheard two men in conversation about church growth problems.

The first man stated: "If we only had a new church building, then we could grow." (Now I believe a new building will attract attention and cause some folk to start attending. I also believe that if we put all our hopes in one project, we may be disappointed.)

The second man disagreed with his friend: "If we did not have this new building and the debt involved, then we could grow!"

Facilities do play a role in church growth, but facility problems can be overcome.

A common problem concerning facilities is over-crowding. It's a *good* problem to have, but it can cause a growth slowdown. There is a law that states: "When you reach 80 percent of capacity in your most crowded area, you may expect a slowdown in the growth rate." Many churches experience over-crowding in their educational space first. This can sometimes be alleviated by dual scheduling or by using alternate sites. Some churches have found that, in addition to Sunday scheduling, another weeknight or Saturday will work for the education hour.

The second problem in the area of facilities is parking. Most growing churches will sooner or later have parking problems. Having just enough spaces to meet city or county zoning requirements is not enough. The average American, used to the ample parking of the shopping mall, will not look very long for a space without growing disinterested. Some churches are finding that parking is now as important, if not more important, than buildings.

If parking is a problem, what can be done? One solution is to buy more land. If it is available and reasonable, land is an excellent long-range investment. (One note: If you invest in land to alleviate parking space problems, go ahead and blacktop the parking area. You will get more efficient use of it and there will be room for more cars when the area has been striped and marked.)

Suppose no land is available or the cost is unreasonable. You may have to improvise. One church facing a parking problem did just that. They set aside 10 spaces directly in front of the church and marked them, "Visitors." Although members may not enjoy hunting for a space, they probably will not give up and leave. But a first-time visitor might.

Another church instituted a park-and-ride program. They received permission from a bank to park cars on the bank's lot on Sundays. Members were asked to drive to the bank, where they were picked up by buses running every few minutes to the church.

Parking need not be a hindrance if a church really wants to grow.

One last problem concerning facilities involves the use of existing buildings. I have been in situations, both as a pastor and as a guest, where space was not being properly used. If, for example, you have a traditional class meeting in a large room such as the main auditorium, while another class of 35 is crowded into a small room, space is probably not being used to its best advantage. Some changes should be made. This may not be easy, but it could become necessary for growth to continue. Efficient and well-planned classrooms can make smaller space meet a growing congregation's needs until the church can build again.

Location

If people cannot find the church, or getting to it is difficult, it may be hard to reach new people. I pastored a small church once that had many positive things going for it. It had a new building on 5 lovely acres. The only problem I could see was location. It was on a dead-end street. The last one-half mile was gravel road. The land had been purchased at a reasonable price, but the location was the greatest liability (they have since moved to more accessible property).

Churches used to look for a nice, quiet street on which to build. But those shaded, tree-lined streets may not be seen by a large percentage of the population. Prime locations include: the area near a shopping center; acreage running along-side a freeway (make sure there is an access road to or near the church); or downtown areas that are coming alive again. You may wish to check with the city, county, or state planning commission concerning new roads or buildings for the future.

Organizational Structure

We have already discussed the need for a growth-oriented structure. It is a prerequisite for growth. If our structure is designed for maintenance, it will produce a negative growth reaction.

Consider the following questions: "What percentage of your budget is directed toward outreach? What percentage toward maintenance? Have you added new groups (Royal Rangers, Missionettes, Sunday school classes) to your structure this year? Do you have a plan for incorporating newcomers into church life? Do you provide a new members' class?"

A flexible structure that allows for growth will give room to expand both ministries and people. An organizational structure designed to maintain the present facilities, budget, etc., will limit growth opportunities.

Role Change for the Pastor

I saw a sign in a barber shop recently that stated: "Everything that grows, changes." While this sign may have been talking about hair, the same words apply to the church. The growing church will go through many changes. As the church expands and grows, so must the pastor. The same qualities that caused the church to grow from 40 to 200 people could hinder or slow down growth from that point on. The pastor and the church members must recognize the changes that naturally take place as the church starts to grow.

First, the pastor will have less time for casual visitors. When the church was smaller, the pastor may have stopped by for a visit or coffee. Now many things compete for his time. Staff meetings, budget discussions, counseling sessions, and other matters demand the pastor's time. These matters tend to cut the pastor off from personal contact with members. Both the pastor and the congregation must realize this and work to keep communications open.

Second, the pastor will delegate ministry to others. In a growing situation, the pastor will often make an effort to visit all the sick, be at every activity, and lead every committee. As the church grows larger, this becomes impossible. Associate ministers or gifted lay persons will assume greater leadership roles. This may cause some to say that the pastor is not as involved as he once was. The pastor must cope with seeing other ministries grow and realize approval by the congregation. As the church grows, he must be willing to "let go" of some of his former duties. Failure to understand the pastoral role change can cause frustration for the pastor as well as confusion and disappointment to the members.

Nonacceptance

Incorporating new members into the body is vital to the life of any church. Failure to accept the newcomer may doom the congregation; nonacceptance has a negative effect on church growth.

It has been estimated that over half the adults attending the average Assemblies of God church came into the church as adults. If this is true, there was a time when these adults needed to be accepted and welcomed.

Let's consider some of the reasons for nonacceptance:

1. Job security is threatened. Some members might think, "If our church grows, then I will not be as important as I once was." Individuals may feel threatened about their future opportunities to minister. It is generally true that as a church grows, *more* opportunities of service are made available.

2. Large churches are unfriendly. This is simply not true. I have been in small and large churches that were warm and friendly. I have also visited

large and small churches that were involved in cliques and were unfriendly. Size has nothing to do with warmth and acceptance.

3. "Those kind of people" will wreck the church. God hates prejudice. While it is a generally accepted fact that people tend to group together in homogeneous groups, all peoples (including racial and ethnic minorities) should feel free to worship in our church.

I was pastoring in southeast Missouri. We had just completed renovating our church. Lovely new carpeting, padded pews, and new lighting made the building a beautiful house of worship. We had an active bus ministry, and many children attended our church without their parents. One Sunday morning, an individual came to me with a strange request: "Get rid of those dirty, little kids. They are soiling our new carpet and wearing out our church!" Now I have to admit that I was not thrilled about the dirt on the carpet. But those children as well as others were our reason for being. Needless to say, this misguided soul left our fellowship.

Our building will never be "people proof." We can afford the paint and the vacuum cleaner. Everyone must be made to feel welcome.

4. "They don't meet our standards." Most sinners won't. But after they get saved, the Lord will have a chance to develop their lives.

People who are different from us may come into our church. They may not live the way we live. They may not dress the way we want them to dress. But God loves them and we must love them too. Trying to make sinners conform to our standards before they are saved could drive them away from God.

As we preach, pray, and give wise counsel this growth hindrance can be overcome.

Knowing How to Get There

Many men and women today have a sincere desire to see growth in the church. Their biggest frustration, however, is not knowing how to reach their goals. They have heard the growth story of the church of 500 or 1,000. They may have heard sessions on multiple-staff relations. But these folk are frustrated in their attempt to reach the first 100! It is necessary, then, to find a proper starting place. The following are suggestions to help remove hindrances to local church growth:

1. Know what kind of church you are. Are you a front-door or side-door church? Why?

2. Evaluate the growth performance of the last 5 years. Did your church growth come from biological, transfer, or conversion growth?

3. Define clear growth goals.

4. Determine what percentage of the budget is spent on maintenance and what percentage is spent on outreach.

5. Could your facilities be used in a more space-efficient manner? If so, how?

6. What attitudes or actions must be changed in order to reach and incorporate the newcomer?

There will always be obstacles facing the growing church. Some of these obstacles are self-inflicted; others are of a different origin. Most growth obstacles can be overcome with the help of the Holy Spirit. As we plan, pray, investigate, experiment, and change when necessary, the church will continue to show steady and healthy growth.

10

Church Planting

When the 13 colonies declared their independence from England in 1776, there were less than 3,000 churches in America. Today there are more than 300,000 churches in the United States alone. Some people and organizations are saying that there are enough churches in America to reach every level of our population. Is this really true?

Four factors have contributed to this view that church planting is no longer necessary:

1. Superior roadways and rapid transportation, both public and private, have made established meeting houses accessible to people from distant communities.

2. Our struggle to overcome social, cultural, and racial segregation has idealized conglomerate churches and discouraged the planting of new churches in the various segments of society.

3. The present infatuation with "giant churches," for whatever motivation, has caused many leaders to resist the planting of new churches as a threat to their empire.

4. Ecclesiastical détente among American churches in this century has produced something of a religious settlement among the various denominations. Everyone, this mentality suggests, has some

preference. To attempt to win a person to active allegiance to Christ and add him to a congregation different from his preference, or different from the one nearest his home, is unabashedly called "proselyting."

One church growth expert says there are 80 million people in America who do not claim to have any allegiance to a Christian group. If this is true, and figures seem to indicate it is, then America is one of the great mission fields of the world. With the increase in mobility—the average American will move three times in his lifetime—many people are removed from traditional family units. Homogeneous groupings are being broken down. There is a need to plant new churches of all kinds.

Preparation for Church Planting

The established church must cultivate a growth consciousness for new church planting. Steps must be taken to prepare the church to give birth to daughter churches. Three levels of preparation are suggested.

Mental Preparation

It is necessary to develop a mental attitude for planting a new church.

What is our church's missions philosophy? "All churches are missionary-minded." "A church that gives to missions will prosper." While it is true that God will bless a church that is committed to missions, not every church body is committed to missionary giving. In fact, some will give as long as their giving does not affect things too close to home.

The church must go beyond just words and begin to actualize missionary commitment.

The church must take a realistic look at opportunities and limitations. There are social, demographic, and geographic boundaries. It may be impossible for a church to effectively minister to people in a town 50 miles away, no matter how large a bus ministry or television coverage they have. Planting a church could be more efficient, effective, and spiritually productive.

The church must overcome local church shortsightedness. "Why should we help others if we are not strong ourselves?" If the Jerusalem church had felt this way, they would never have left Jerusalem.

A few years ago, Brother Sidney Ramphal left his native country of Guyana, South America, to establish a black home missions church in Kansas City, Missouri. Grace Assembly of God showed beautiful signs of life from its beginning, and with excellent leadership it has become a strong voice in the black community. From the start, Grace Assembly was concerned about missions. They began giving to other missionary works while still receiving assistance themselves. I believe one contributing factor to their growth was their ability to look beyond themselves and see the opportunity to help others.

We must cultivate a winning spirit. God's plan for the Church is growth. The New Testament Church has been called to reproduce itself. It has been said: "A church that expects great things from God can attempt great things for God."

Organizational Preparation

The church must prepare organizationally. Consider the following five guidelines:

1. Make specific assignments in church planting to lay leaders in the congregation. This leadership could come in the form of a local missions committee or a specially organized task force. The purpose of this assignment would be to place responsibility for growth on this level in the local body and not just on the denominational level.

2. Give the church planting committee visibility before the congregation. Kind words and enthusiastic support of an idea will go far in placing approval on their actions.

3. Choose leaders for this committee that have a desire to reach the lost. Their evangelistic fervor must be transmitted to others.

4. Provide training helps and resources for the church planting committee. They need tools and instruction to make their assignment a success.

5. Turn the committee loose to function. Allow them to plan, promote, and enlist others who have specialized talents in church planting.

Practical Preparation

We must prepare the church for a practical role in church planting. It is necessary to secure definite commitment and involvement from members of the local body. Commitment should come in four areas:

1. Prayer—Prayer is necessary in the establishment of any new church. If a church planting opportunity is to be a success, fervency in prayer will be needed. Organized prayer groups should be devoted to this undertaking.

2. Training—As Dr. Melvin Hodges has said, "Most congregations are given to maintenance." It is necessary to think outreach. Training must be

provided in areas of evangelism, outreach, and new church planting. Helps in evaluation, preparation, visitation, small-group worship, and other areas should be given.

3. Money—Money so often becomes the problem in church planting. It is one thing to pray for a new work, but often it is another to take funds that could be used for a new furnace to financially underwrite a new work. It may not be feasible or necessary to totally underwrite a program, but assistance in selected areas will be invaluable. We should remember that money is best spent on people, not things. Do we make a mistake in building a $100,000 building and then paying the pastor $50 a week? Investment in people will pay continuing dividends.

4. People—If a church is really serious about church planting, it will be necessary to invest people—individuals and families—in the new work. One might say, "Giving up people will weaken our own structure." But it seems it was a New Testament pattern for the early churches to become established and then send out key personnel to start new churches. Paul and Barnabas were sent from a church to do just that. If we are to make an impact on America in these last days, it may become necessary for us to increase the number of churches.

Questions to Consider

As we discuss the subject of church planting, additional questions come to mind:

1. "Which church will grow faster, an already established one or a new church with limited resources?" According to a study by Dr. Charles Mylander, representative of the Institute of Ameri-

can Church Growth, newly formed churches will grow faster. The Nazarene church did a study of their church growth from 1906 to 1971. They found that in the beginning (with limited resources) they grew at a much healthier pace than at the end of their survey. They also noted that growth came during periods when they planted large numbers of churches.

The Assemblies of God has had good success in planting new churches. According to Clarence Lambert, secretary of New Church Evangelism:

> The 1980s have been declared by our Movement as the decade of church planting. The Assemblies of God is mobilizing for a formal thrust in new church evangelism. My hope is that we will increase in church planting by one third as we near the end of this decade. (This statement was made during a personal interview in November 1980.)

2. "When you talk about planting new churches, aren't you really talking about unholy competition? Don't we have enough competition between churches and denominations today?" Wendall Belew, of the Southern Baptist Home Missions Board, in *Church Growth America* magazine (vol. 1, #4) states:

> Two churches are more complementary than competitive. Two churches minister to people of two different mind sets, two different cultural inclinations. They will reach twice as many unchurched as one will. We need not be afraid of competition between local churches and denominations.

3. "How large should a church be before it plants another church?" That will depend on the thinking of the congregation and other local circumstances.

Some feel that if a church has a building it should think of planting another church.

Herbert C. Peak, Jr., pastor of First Assembly of God in Georgetown, South Carolina, has recently joined the ranks of church planters. Brother Peak and his congregation felt a burden for a small town approximately 30 miles from Georgetown. They considered busing or an outstation ministry. None of these ideas seemed practical for the situation. After much prayer and planning they decided to plant a new church.

Georgetown is a town of about 9,000. First Assembly has about 200 adherents. After prayerful consideration, First Assembly gave their assistant pastor and a few families to the new work. They also made a financial commitment to help with a building and pay the new pastor's salary for a period of time. Brother Peak reports that both churches are doing well. As First Assembly gave of itself, new growth more than made up for the losses.

Fallacies About Church Planting

Carroll Nyquist, president of the Johnson Nyquist Film Productions, has participated in a research program on church planting. In an article titled "What Is Sophism?" he stated: "Sophism is an argument, especially a formal one embodying a subtle fallacy, but intended as a blatant deception" (Institute for American Church Growth, Advanced Church Growth Seminar, January 1981).

There are certain sayings that we have heard relating to church growth and church planting that we accept as truth. Mr. Nyquist feels that in the light of God's plan for church growth, these statements (or *sophisms*) are basically false. The following are some examples of sophisms:

1. "Different churches have different purposes. God does not expect or intend for all churches to reach the lost." No statement could be further from the truth. It is God's plan for the church to reach out to lost persons. We must recognize that all persons without Christ are lost, and we are called to bring them the good news.

2. "Quality of members is better than quantity." The natural tendency for a church is to become self-centered. The church growth term used to describe this is *ingrowth*. When we only look inside and seek to better ourselves, the church will probably die within two generations.

3. "The bigger the church, the more effective its ministry." It has been noted that several medium-size churches are generally more effective than one "super church." Often smaller churches exhibit a vitality and determination to grow that forces them to reach out with more excitement than larger ones.

4. "Only large churches should involve themselves in church planting." Donald McGavern made the statement recently: "Any church with its own building and pastor should consider having a daughter church." The need is pressing and the opportunity great. Mother churches often experience additional growth and vitality through the concentrated effort of planting new churches.

5. "American communities are overchurched. Planting new churches is redundant." If the attendance and membership figures of all the churches in a given community were added up and compared with the total population, it would prob-

ably be discovered that a sizable proportion of the population does not attend church. Most communities have large groups of people that have absolutely no significant church contact.

6. "Church planting is a process of developing new churches that are exact miniatures of the 'parent church.' " Many lost persons will not join an established church because there are differences in background, income, or other areas. Possibly the genius behind planting a new church is that it can meet the specialized needs of a local community. It would be a mistake to assume that the new church should be just like the parent church.

God's plan for the Church calls for the New Testament church to reproduce itself. As we give, train, pray, and multiply, the church will grow. Church planting is necessary as we fulfill the Great Commission in these last days.

11

Conserving Church Growth

One of the most exciting and talked-about happenings in any community is the church that starts to grow. People notice extra cars parked in the parking lot. Excitement among neighbors and friends is contagious. A growing, healthy church is a thing of beauty.

Looking at the other side of the picture, however, nothing is as pitiful as a church that has lost its momentum. Maintaining church growth is a vital concern to all who are a part of the body of Christ. Some churches seem to rise and fall with the changing seasons. This is not in God's plan for the Church. Steps can be taken to preserve church growth within the body. Consider the following ingredients which are vital to the preservation of the existing church.

Leadership

We will deal with leadership on both the pastoral and the lay level in chapter 12. Pastoral leadership, however, is an integral ingredient in preserving church growth today. The pastor is a key person in developing the personality of the church. If he is friendly and outgoing, church members will tend to be like him. His conscious efforts to lead a congregation in warmth and acceptance of newcomers will be copied by others.

Flexibility

This word could be used to describe the desire to accommodate the needs of your community. You must make a special effort in your united outreach to people. Flexibility is also needed to maintain fellowship with the newcomer and continued service to the member of long-standing. Flexibility should not be misunderstood as suggesting change. Changing something just for the sake of change is not a good reason.

Flexibility says: "Without compromising the integrity or standard of the church, we will adapt, change, and do whatever is necessary to meet the needs of all our people."

Rev. Ray Corlew is the pastor of a growing Assembly of God in Grand Forks, North Dakota. He described an outreach opportunity that is helping his congregation to maintain excellent growth in their area. The church had just finished a building program, but already they were crowded. Should they build again so soon? Instead of expanding their facilities, they decided to look in another direction. Grand Forks is near a military base, and many of the Christians stationed there have duties that tie them to their jobs on Sunday. Brother Corlew and the Grand Forks Assembly started a "Saturday school" to meet their needs. Some of these folk could not have attended on Sunday. Saturday worked better for them, and it also alleviated the space problem at the same time. In preserving growth, the church was saying, "We care for you and your families."

The growing church needs an organizational structure, growth goals, and a sense of direction. It also must be flexible and sensitive enough to flow with the needs, and sometimes the desires, of its people.

Staff Training

A great contributor to consistent church growth is a well-trained and committed staff. We have learned the hard way that just getting people to church and Sunday school is not enough. They must be fed once they arrive. Anything less will cause spiritual starvation and a deterioration of the program.

Training is essential to maintain church growth and should be conducted on all levels.

1. Sunday school—In recent years, the national Sunday School Department has placed great emphasis on training. Workers training programs, the workers training book-of-the-year, the staff training series (this is a new program to help the leader in workers conferences), and teachers' certification have played an important part in the effort to better train teachers and workers. The *Sunday School Counselor* offers training helps with a monthly Leader Edition.

The Sunday school that wants to grow and maintain growth will do so as trained and well-equipped staff members minister with confidence. As learning brings change in the students' lives, the church will grow.

2. Total-church training—With the advent of the

church growth movement, all-church training has found its place. Church growth seminars, lay leadership institutes, and other programs involve the entire church in studying methods of outreach.

3. Youth, men's, and women's ministries—These departments of the church can provide excellent training opportunities. With the help of the national headquarters, they can offer specialized training for leadership and group members.

Qualitative Instruction

Closely related to the training of the staff is the quality and type of instruction the students receive. Students are no longer content to be passive learners. They want to participate and be involved in the teaching plans. Growing churches are using a variety of teaching methods in the Sunday school and in other educational areas to keep interest and maintain quality programs.

Secular education has taught us that when students are actively involved in the session, they will learn more and retain information for longer periods. Techniques such as class discussion, role-playing, audiovisuals, drama, agree-disagree statements, and other methods are being used today. These involvement opportunities help maintain a higher level of interest.

Facilities

We have mentioned facilities in an earlier chapter. While we recognize that facilities must not be used as an excuse to keep from growing, how well we use our facilities may determine whether or not we grow. Many churches are now looking at the multipurpose building as the first stage of their building program. Multipurpose buildings are also helpful additions to older, less functional buildings. Often the multipurpose building will have a kitchen, fellowship hall, and other activity space that requires little set-up time for use. With the high cost of buildings today and the increase in family ministries, the multipurpose building could be an excellent growth tool.

Fellowship

"Ours is a friendly church." Most people like to think this is true of their church. Your church probably is a friendly church. However, at times this can be our greatest liability. You say, "How can this be? We're supposed to be friendly." Suppose you come to the church on Sunday morning. You have not seen your church family since Wednesday night. Maybe the children have had the flu or Aunt Martha has died. Something good may have happened. There is so much to talk about. Maybe we get so busy sharing with one another that others are left out of our conversation. It is important that everyone be included in fellowship.

Motivation

Motivation is a key to continued success in the local church. We must motivate members to keep them participating in worship and ministry. We must motivate workers to keep them involved.

One church growth expert has suggested that the 10 strongest factors in motivating people are:

1. Appetite
2. Love and concern for their offspring

3. Health
4. Sexual attraction
5. Parental affection
6. Ambition
7. Pleasure
8. Bodily comfort
9. Possessions
10. Approval of others

It is interesting to note that a number of the items listed here may also affect the church as it attempts to minister to people. Some additional observations about people can be made:

1. People are more interested in themselves than in anyone else.
2. People are interested in new things.
3. People are easily confused.
4. People are important.
5. People forget quickly and need to be reminded.
6. People find it hard to remember words.
7. People find it easier to remember pictures.
8. People's emotions are more powerful than their minds.
9. People will be moved when they have vision.
10. People want to be happy.
11. People basically want to be good.

The church is in the community to minister to people. How we affect them and motivate them, both to work and respond, may tell if we succeed or fail.

"We Care" Program

If the church is to maintain present growth and

continue to reach out to new opportunities, it must say to the community, "We care." Nowadays, when people are afraid to let their true feelings show, a caring program is most important. There are four strategic areas of caring and ministry for a concerned, local church:

1. Identifying receptive people and their needs.
2. Responding to these needs in a unique way through the church.
3. Reaching and assimilating these new people into active membership in the church.
4. Nurturing new members into long-term, active fellowship in the church.

Giving attention to the church's caring system—with all its ministries, programs, and groups—will enable the church to significantly improve the quality of its ministry, outreach, and discipleship to the people in the community.

As we seek to become a caring body we must discover effective ways of locating and reaching receptive, potential new members in our community. We must further examine the important ingredients for making our church a caring church that is capable of responding to the needs of people around us. We must begin developing building blocks for an effective new-member recruitment and church growth program. We must examine the important roles of the pastor and lay person in developing our caring system. We must strengthen our personal faith and relationship to Christ.

A caring system involves:

1. Knowing those you want to reach and why you want to reach them.

2. Knowing the needs of those you desire to reach.

3. Knowing the entry events and entry paths where new persons are most likely to be met, welcomed, and introduced to your church and fellowship.

4. Matching the needs of each person with a task-role or group opportunity to assure continued acceptance, belonging, and growing faith.

5. Continuing to monitor, manage, and guide the involvement of each new member, assuring the development of his faith and his spiritual growth.

6. Adopting new persons into existing groups, and alerting groups and leaders to their ministry of caring.

7. Adding new groups and programs to meet the needs of the persons you wish to reach.

8. Multiplying the entry events and entry paths; opening the church at every possible point to potential new members.

Maintaining church growth is not an easy task. It involves committed leadership, growth goals, and vision. The healthy, alive, constantly growing church must exercise faith, demonstrate concern, and realize proper motivation.

God's plan for the Church requires us to nurture and disciple those in our charge while reaching out to lost persons.

12

The Role of Leadership in the Church

The city was somewhere in the central United States and the date was 1975. First Assembly of God was losing members. Its losses had been consistent over the years. An excellent location, an adequate building and parking area, and a flow of people from the metropolitan area had given every natural opportunity to grow a healthy church. But instead of growth, this church was dying spiritually, numerically, and financially.

Now it was 3 years later—1978. It was a providential year for this assembly. New leadership, both on the pastoral and lay level, sought God for growth. In a matter of months, this struggling congregation rose from its deathbed to new life. Today, its vital signs are good. The church is rapidly becoming a picture of health. Leadership—both lay and pastoral—does make a difference. This is not to say the church's former leaders were not of God. But a change in leadership was evident.

In the following pages we will consider pastoral leadership, lay people in leadership roles, and the local church as a leader in the community.

First, let's consider the pastor. What effect does he have on the growth of the church?

A young man was interviewing the pastor of a

growing church. He made the statement: "This church is really wonderful. How did you happen to get a great church like this?" The pastor smiled and responded, "I got a great church like this with about 18 hours a day of hard work!" A person usually does not "fall" into a great situation. It comes from hard work. A pastor with church growth leadership potential will possess many God-given growth attributes. The following is a partial list of those attributes.

Commitment to God

If a man is going to lead others, he must be sure of his calling and commitment to God. If I *think* that God and I have a working agreement, but I'm not *convinced* of that arrangement, it can easily be shaken. I must be sure of my commitment to God and His commitment to me.

When I first began pastoring, I quickly learned it was not as easy a job as I had assumed. Preparing sermons and keeping office hours were only part of the pressure. About 1 year after becoming involved in full-time ministry, I developed serious bleeding ulcers. I could not eat or sleep. During that time I ate enough cottage cheese and chipped beef to last a lifetime. My doctor advised me that the ministry might be putting me under too much pressure. He even suggested that I might not be suited to the rigors of the pastorate and should consider another type of employment.

I sought the advice of an elder minister in whom I had much confidence. He asked me, "Do you know that you are called?" "Yes," I replied, "I know I am." He advised me, "You must be worrying about things that God didn't intend for you to worry about. Why don't you do the worrying during the daytime and let God do the worrying at night."

That sounds simple, but I learned that if I was committed to God, the work could also be committed to Him. One Scripture passage that made an impact on my life at this time comes from Paul's writings: "For I know whom I have believed, and am persuaded that he is able to keep that which I have committed unto him against that day" (2 Timothy 1:12).

Commitment is a two-way street between you and God. (The Lord healed the ulcers about the time I understood my commitment to Him.)

On another occasion, the church I was pastoring was involved in a building program and finances were really tight. During this trial, Isaiah 43:1-3 came alive to me:

> Fear not: for I have redeemed thee, I have called thee by thy name; thou art mine. When thou passest through the waters, I will be with thee; and through the rivers, they shall not overflow thee: when thou walkest through the fire, thou shalt not be burned; neither shall the flame kindle upon thee. For I am the LORD thy God.

What a comfort to realize that God knows my name! Just as I am committed to God, He is committed to me.

Love for God's People

We love all of God's people, yet God gives a special love to the church growth pastor for his community.

Tommy Barnett, former pastor of Westside

Assembly of God in Davenport, Iowa, related his first impression of the city in which God was to use him so mightily: "I thought Davenport was a cold, ugly, and dirty city." It was the last place on earth that Brother Barnett would have chosen to pioneer a church. But God gave him a love for that city and its people. That love brought a ripe harvest to the entire region. As God gives gifts, He will place love in the pastor's heart for his people.

The Ability to Communicate

The church growth pastor must communicate on two levels. First, he must effectively communicate the Word of God, touching lives for Christ. Second, he must communicate in practical terms to his staff and congregation his hopes, dreams, goals, and direction for the ministry of the church. Communication is a great asset to the church growth pastor.

Motivation

The church growth pastor/leader must motivate and involve lay persons in the work. Since volunteer workers are not members of the staff, the time and resources that they can give are often limited. Job and family needs must not be neglected. Usually volunteers are more willing to commit themselves for a short term rather than an indefinite period of time.

Volunteers should not be taken for granted. They need to be appreciated and encouraged. Public recognition for a job well done will tell a volunteer of his worth to the congregation. Gentle, courteous treatment will spare hurt feelings and allow the individual to minister again another day.

Consistency in Attitude and Action

The word *predictability* could also be used here. The lay person must know how the pastor/leader will react to certain situations. If the pastor is on the mountaintop one day and low in the valley the next, those highs and lows might discourage someone from approaching him with a need or problem. The pastor/leader who can find a level of consistency will be more approachable.

The pastor/leader is a key to growth in the church. As he remains constant, gentle in spirit, committed to God, loving, and communicative, he will lead the congregation in growth.

The lay person also has a key role in leadership. He, too, must be committed to God and aware of God's acceptance of him. There are other qualities of leadership the lay person must also consider:

1. Loyalty—This loyalty is to the Lord, the church, and the pastor. He must recognize that he represents all of these. The lay person's leadership testimony will be a blessing or a hindrance to the community's attitude toward the church.

2. Commitment to training—In many cases, the lay leader, though well qualified in his own profession, will not have had training in church growth. To be a good teacher, he must be a good learner. More training is available for lay leaders today than ever before. A wise lay person in a leadership role will make use of every training opportunity.

3. Commitment to the newcomer—The lay leader can either feel threatened by the newcomer and resent him, or make him feel warm and accepted. Leadership on this level will affect all members of the church and their relationship to new people.

4. Commitment to stewardship—Just as a pastor/leader must be a good steward, so the lay leader must be a good steward of time, talent, and money. His life must be an example to the rest of the congregation.

5. Commitment to the lost—We cannot place a price on souls. Whatever the cost, the lay leader must share this burden with the pastoral staff.

Church leadership can be broken down into five classes, three of which affect the lay person:

Class 1 leadership—Members in the church whose energies primarily turn inward toward maintenance of the organizational structure of the church.

Class 2 leadership—Members of the church whose energies primarily turn outward toward the non-Christian community in an effort to bring them into the body of Christ.

Class 3 leadership—Members in the church who are partially paid and whose activities are divided between the church and outside activities.

Class 4 leadership—Individuals in the church who are full-time, paid personnel and viewed as professional staff.

Class 5 leadership—Denominational, district, or administrative personnel, usually removed from the immediate scene of the local church.

It should be noted that of all the classes of leadership, classes 1, 2, and 3 will have the most direct contact with the greatest potential for growth for the church. It should be further noted that the key to dynamic, effective church growth will in most cases be found in the recruiting, training, and utilizing of class 2 workers.

Pastoral and lay leadership must work together as a team. When they are united in a spiritual marriage, they will contribute to growth.

Leadership in the Community

A church must be committed to leadership in the community. Every city, town, or rural area seemingly has one church that becomes the spiritual leader in its ministry area.

In the 1980s, many of these ministry areas will again be served by an Assemblies of God church. I am not suggesting that we become the watchdog for the entire community. Neither am I suggesting that the church attempt to exercise undue or improper influence on business or politics. Fear tactics will not serve the church well. I do believe that the Church can, by speaking according to God's Word, be an effective conscience. In this and in other areas we must accept responsibility. The dynamic Pentecostal church will assume leadership in the community by:

1. Reaching the lost. This is still a priority. Our greatest concern must be that the lost are really lost and that there is salvation through Jesus Christ.

2. Providing Christian education for the church and the world. We must make a commitment to teach all the commandments (as Jesus commanded in the Great Commission).

3. Improving the quality of life. Not necessarily through social programs, but indirectly as a result of the higher standard of living enjoyed by the believer. (Consider the rights and privileges of a Christian weighed against the habits and problems brought upon the unbeliever by sin.)

4. Providing fellowship for the Body.

5. Ministering to the members of the Body. As we look outward, we must not neglect those within the Body.

The Church is alive and well. Thousands upon thousands are looking to the Church for leadership in the 1980s. As pastor and lay persons unite with Christ to be the Church, God's plan will be fulfilled.

13

Paying the Price

"Church growth does not come cheaply. It carries a price tag. Both pastor and people must be willing to pay the price for growth" (C. Peter Wagner).

What is the cost of church growth today? Who will ultimately pay the price for growth? The price must be paid on two levels: first, by the pastor, and second, by the congregation.

The Pastor

Willing to Work Hard

The pastor must be committed to hard work. If he is leading a growing church, time, both private and in ministry, will be at a premium. Pastoring the growing church will drain the minister physically, mentally, and spiritually. It will become necessary for him to stretch his creative energy to the limit. Decisions, meetings, problems, and people will demand his time. The pastor of the growing church will move from one crossroads to another. Not everyone will be willing to sacrifice time, energy, and personal resources to be involved in a growing situation.

The pastor must make up his mind to grow. He must believe that it is God's will for his church to grow. When he comes to this conclusion, he will do whatever is necessary to help the church reach out in growth. The church will not grow without commitment and hard work. In most cases, the benefits will far outweigh the drawbacks.

As the church growth pastor sees lives changed and the church grow strong, the excitement and blessing will sustain him in his work.

Willing to Be a Student

The pastor must continue to be a student of church growth. Many exciting and wonderful things are happening in the area of church growth. Learning opportunities, now more than at any other time, are available to the pastor. Church growth books, seminars, evaluations, and other programs will help him understand, diagnose, and prepare a plan of action for his church. As the pastor is willing to become a student, he will be equipped to teach his "church family" concerning the growth that is to come.

Willing to Put His Leadership on the Line

The pastor must be willing to put his own leadership on the line. Planning and goal setting give direction to the congregation, but can also point out failures. The pastor puts himself and his ministry on the line when he dares to reach out in growth.

I remember the first time I ever set a goal as a pastor. My church was averaging approximately 50 in Sunday school. I had attended a Sunday school convention where the speaker had said, "Don't set a goal unless it scares you!" A goal of 75 people in

Sunday school didn't scare me. We had seen almost 70 a few weeks before. So, we set a goal of 100 people in attendance for the Sunday before Christmas.

When my wife heard about the goal she did her best to comfort me. The Sunday school superintendent said, "It's a great idea, but should we really tell the people?" But I made the announcement in church: "With God's help we are going to have 100 people in Sunday school on the Sunday before Christmas."

I must give the congregation credit. They worked very hard. As pastor I was confident that we would reach our goal, but the Saturday night before the big day I said to myself, "What if we don't make it?" Failure would be a personal mark on my leadership. I needn't have worried. We had 110 in Sunday school! God gave us 10 percent more than we had asked for.

A lesson was learned from this experience. As a leader, I was responsible to a certain extent for the success or failure of our outreach. There was a risk in my reaching out. The church growth pastor must be willing to place himself in the line of fire, as he makes public his place in God's plan for growth.

Willing to Share Leadership

The church growth pastor must be willing to share leadership. We have already discussed the role of the leader. Some pastors do have difficulty, however, in sharing responsibility. One man, depending on his natural talents and energy, can effectively pastor a church of 150 or so adherents. As the church continues to grow, however, his personal contact with the people will diminish. Additional staff members or lay leaders will have to pick up some of the work load. This may cause the pastor, and even some members, to feel that he is not doing his job. He will not have the same contact that he had in the early days of his ministry. For this reason, the pastor may be unwilling or hesitant to "give up" part of his congregation to someone else.

The pastor must be willing to share leadership. He must be willing to see others prosper within his ministry area. Lay leaders and associate ministers will become extensions of the pastor. This growth necessity may be a high price to pay for some men.

Willing to Commit Himself

The church growth pastor must be willing to commit himself to his people. Pastoral longevity is being recognized more and more as a church growth ingredient. In a survey of the 115 fastest-growing Assemblies of God churches in the United States, many responding pastors gave tenure in office as a strong contributor to growth. Consider the following reasons:

1. Longevity increases knowledge of the needs of the people. It is impossible to be aware of the congregation's needs collectively or individually in 1 year of ministry. Some ministerial relationships take a longer time to develop. If the pastor is to effectively give of himself, he must be aware of the needs of his people.

2. Longevity builds confidence. Can I really trust this man? Will he betray my confidence? In most cases the pastor is very trustworthy. However, it does take time to build trust and confidence.

3. Longevity produces continuity in planning.

Every individual is different. Each pastor will run his program in his own way. If a congregation changes pastors every 2 years, they will be constantly shifting their emphasis. A 5- or 10-year plan of action will be helpful to the growth of the church. This can only come with a pastor's longevity.

4. Longevity builds community relations. People in the community watch the pastor and his congregation. If a church changes pastors every year or two that could seem disruptive. Longevity builds business and community relations that will go far in contributing to the growth of the church.

There is a price to pay in commitment to a group of people. From time to time, so-called "greener pastures" will appear. The church growth pastor must consider this and other factors as he counts the cost. Some may find that the necessities for growth mentioned on these pages cost too much. Church growth does have a price to be paid by the pastor.

The Congregation

Church growth also involves a cost to the congregation. The church body must be willing to pay the price if they are to see lasting growth.

One church had every opportunity to grow. In talking with members, I got the impression of a committed, caring congregation. They meant well, but hard facts showed they were unwilling to pay the price. They let their building become a monument rather than a gathering place for souls. They would give to a party fund, but not to missions. They showed mistrust for the pastor and other full-time staff members. The end result was the sin of ingrowth. They looked inward, neglecting the mission field around them. One member made the statement after several newcomers had decided not to join, "At least now I don't have to hunt for a place to sit!" This church is dying because it is unwilling to pay the price for growth.

If the church is to grow, it must stretch itself to its limits in four areas.

Finances

The church must be willing to provide dollars for growth. Money, or the use of money, has more than once been a drawback to church growth. With the growth of the church, expenses will rise. Many times in the early stages of growth, monetary expenses will develop far quicker than the return brought about by new people. Space requirements, additional parking, equipment, curriculum materials, extra staff members, and other expenses may place some pressure on a church body.

The church must decide to spend for outreach. Too much of the budget may be allocated to maintenance. We must ask ourselves the question: "How high a price are we willing to pay for church growth?" With escalating building costs, high interest rates, and energy needs, the church will have to determine what price it will pay for growth.

Leadership

The church must be willing to follow a growth leader. Too many times a pastor catches a vision of growth only to find that his congregation is resistive to change. The congregation must believe in the man God has sent to them. They must be willing to move with God's man as he experiments with the growth mix available to him.

Personal Commitment

The church must be willing to give time and energy for growth. Church growth does not just happen. While we realize that the anointing of the Spirit of God is vital to any growing, healthy church, time and effort will be required of the members. It is not enough to give money. Church growth stewardship involves giving of ourselves. One area of commitment could involve a local church growth committee. They would be responsible for informing and motivating lay persons. They would study, pray, plan, promote, and lead in outreach programs. This would require a weekly investment of time.

Some church members may quickly reply that the pastor is to do the work. But the church growth individual will accept a responsible position of ministry alongside the pastor. This person will be giving something very special. He will be giving himself.

Fellowship

The church must be willing to sacrifice fellowship. Many who are willing to give, pray, and promote for growth will do everything necessary to grow but this one thing. They do not want to lose close fellowship with everyone in the church. In a church of 50 to 100 persons, everyone probably knows each other. Often, needs and other information about members' lives is also known. But when a church grows it becomes impossible to know everyone.

Some people may be afraid the church will be overrun by strangers. While fellowship is desired, the church must realize that as growth occurs, there will be groups and subgroups in fellowship. These groups will be diversified, but tied by a common bond in Christ.

If the church is to grow, there is a price to pay. The pastor will have to give of himself. He will, in one sense, have to give his family to a community. He will have to give some of his dreams and future ambitions. The church growth pastor will, ultimately, have to give his life for his church.

The congregation must respond in like fashion—giving time, talents, and money. The church must not only seek to maintain, but also be willing to risk its individual and collective feelings to grow.

The pastor and the congregation are a ministry team. As they together pay the price, the church will grow.

A Final Thought

Church growth has come to God's kingdom for such a time as this. The wind of the Holy Spirit is spreading the seed of church growth across the land. As the world faces even greater trials, the Church will continue to shine as a light in the world. As men and women struggle in helplessness as lost persons, the Church must continue to reach out in salvation.

God has a plan for the Church. God's plan for the Church is growth—growth through winning the lost to Christ and nurturing believers in the faith!

A CIRCUS OF BLOOD

Stranger Blaine Devereaux has big plans for Quirt. He's putting the godforsaken town on the map by turning a buffalo hunt into a bloody carnival event. Now trigger-happy folks from miles around are drawn to Quirt for the savage competition. It's also drawing Matt Ramsey. But he's hunting for something else … a sinister conspiracy to gain control of prime Indian territory. Smooth-talking Devereaux isn't above killing off the buffalo to get what he wants—and he's marked Matt Ramsey for extinction as well.…

FOR GENERATIONS THEY HAVE SURVIVED. BRAVE, STURDY, AND STRONG-WILLED, THE RAMSEYS HAVE FORGED OUT A RUGGED NEW LIFE IN NORTH TEXAS, OVERCOMING DROUGHT, DISEASE, AND THE MAYHEM OF THE CIVIL WAR. UNITED BY THEIR BLOOD, EVERY RAMSEY IS BORN TO FIGHT FOR JUSTICE AND FREEDOM ON THE AMERICAN FRONTIER. THIS IS THEIR STORY.

10525>

0 71152 00295 2

ISBN 0-515-10525-2